It is a sad but true fact that those who make history seldom write it. Possibly the struggle for existence is often so strenuous that no opportunity is found to record the daily events which go to make up history for the succeeding generations. Perhaps, too, the events that seem so important to those of us who live in this age were ordinary and everyday occurrences to those who enacted them. The romance and adventure which we find in piercing the veil that hides the early history of Blair County was, no doubt, to those who made this history, simply a struggle to eke out an existence. That their efforts were successful, cannot be denied; that the foundations they laid were solid, needs no proof; that they worked with a vision of the future greatness of this quaint section of Pennsylvania can be seen in all that they accomplished under the most trying circumstances. The value of history is in its inspiration and example to succeeding generations. The love and pride which we have in our little town, our genealogies, and our possessions spring in the most part from noble lives and works of those who cleared the paths of life upon which our feet now tread. We glory in their accomplishments and profit by their mistakes.

The years have been kind to Newry. No great changes have taken place to detract from its serenity and the beauty of its surroundings. And, too, the early days still live in the perpetuation of the old family names as one generation succeeds another.

Rev. Jeremiah P. Flynn

(from the writings of Father Flynn)

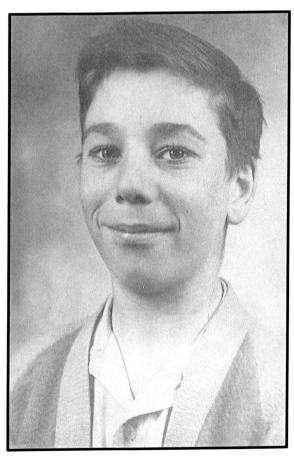

Francis "Hezzie" Thompson
1945

These writings are dedicated to my wife, Charleen, who has endured much for the past fifty- eight years with this "good ole" Newry boy.

Thank you for your patience and understanding over the past many years.

And thanks to the good Lord for allowing me the time to complete this journal.

Charleen, "You are the wind beneath my wings."

The Thompson Children

Audrey . . . . *May 4, 1916*
Roger (Jake) . . . . *April 2, 1926*
Raymond . . . . *March 30, 1928*
Phyllis (Phitty) . . . . *October 6, 1929*
Francis (Hezzie) . . . . . *January 12, 1932*
Paul (Popeye) . . . . *July 22, 1934*
Joseph . . . . *July 14, 1936*
James . . . . *August 29, 1937*
Robert (Dewey) . . . . *March 28, 1939*
Eugene (Butch) . . . . *December 19, 1941*
Donald (Babe) . . . . *May 2, 1943*
Rita (Honey) . . . . *August 24, 1945*

FORWARD

Quite a few years ago, while joking with some friends from the "big town" of Newry, Pennsylvania, I threatened to one day write a book about our "growing up years".

The opportunity to attempt this project came at an unexpected time, through an injury I suffered in the winter of 1998-99. I was experiencing severe cramping in my left foot and leg and sought relief from a young orthopedic surgeon, Dr. David Welker, at the Blair Orthopedic medical offices in Altoona. At my first appointment I told the doctor how I would get up at night and slide out of bed to the floor, put my left leg up against the wall and cry a bit. After a half-hour or so, the pain would ease up and I would go back to bed. The doctor explained in long medical terminology what my problem was and how to fix it.

As we were discussing my situation, Dr. Greg Fulchiero, another talented resident surgeon and a former Newry boy came by and stopped to say hello. He knew well "Hezzie" Thompson and inquired as to my injury. Without hesitation, he told my doctor, "He's old" and walked away.

The long and short of this ordeal was an operation that fused three or four of my toes, taking away forever my dream of becoming a professional tap dancer. The recovery period took about five months, necessitating therapy and the wearing of the most uncomfortable straight jacket of a boot for several months. What hurt the most, though, was the loss of my hunting and fishing "privileges".

Winter turned to spring during my recuperative period and I was able to retreat to the back porch where I enjoyed a constant stream of visitors. It was on one of these occasions, that Allie, the youngest of my eight grandchildren, suggested, "Pap, why don't we write a story?"

And so it began. We would write a paragraph or so every time she would come to visit. One day after she went home I was looking over some of the stories and decided to start a journal of my early years in Newry.

I took the idea of writing this journal to some friends and was encouraged by their response. As time went by, more people found out about my little project and graciously contributed a few of their own stories.

Now, of course, when I run into them at various functions such as the annual St. Patrick's Festival, the yearly Lenten fish fry in Newry, or on more solemn occasions at Sorge's Funeral Home, they always ask, "Hezzie, how's your book coming along?"

Having committed to writing about the good old days in Newry, a few disclaimers follow —

These writings are informal, in no certain order, and not guaranteed to be absolutely factual, as some are shared a few times removed from the original actors and events. I, as the writer, dare not question the "authenticity" of said events, participants, or providers of the facts. As any true "Newryite" will attest…everything gets better with age.

Growing up in a small town like Newry had certain

advantages. You knew the name of everyone in town, along with their dogs, cats, and rabbits if they had them. It is from this intimacy that these writings have sprung; some comical, some sad, but all an integral part of our early years.

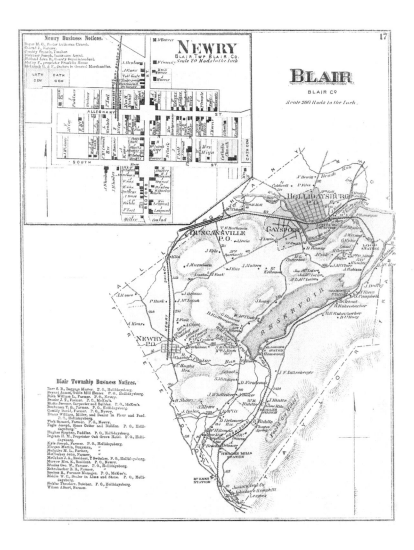

THE EARLY YEARS

My earliest recollection of life in Newry started when we lived in the old Homer Glunt house that sat next to Piney McCoy's bar, also known as the "Franklin House."

The Glunt House

One day when I was about four or five years old and playing beside our house, I found a large metal nut and tied it to a piece of string. I remember it made a neat noise as I swung it 'round and 'round, little knowing that as I did, the string wore thinner and thinner. A very large picture window fronted our dining room, and wouldn't you know it, that string broke and the nut went right through the window!

Well, I wasn't about to stick around and face my mother, so I high-tailed it next door to McCoy's Tavern, crying up a storm. Bertha and Eleanor Lee McCoy took me in and dried my tears as I recounted my story. I don't recall the outcome of this incident, but you can bet I never swung a nut on a string again for the rest of my life!

Living close to McCoy's had a lot of advantages and some of my fondest memories are of the times I spent there. Bertha and Eleanor Lee would take me to Mass at St. Patrick's Catholic Church, and I can still remember leaning my head against one of the big marble pillars

and falling fast asleep.

Looking back, I may have had an ulterior motive for encouraging the friendship with the ladies, as they sold Penn Cress ice cream (the very best!). Bertha would leave some ice cream at the bottom of those two or three gallon containers and somehow I always managed to be there when she was changing them!

There was an old oak bench in front of McCoy's where the old timers used to sit to chew tobacco or smoke their corncob pipes and sometimes "stretch the truth" a bit while sharing their life stories. I always imagined that anyone with any degree of notoriety had his initials hewn into that bench at one time or another. The day that Joe Conrad carved my initials into the bench for me became one of the more memorable in my young life. Joe also bragged that he had the sharpest penknife in Blair County, and I, being a believer...believed him.

When the boys and I sat on the bench we would play a game we called "license plates". The speed limit on the main street in Newry was about fifty back then, and we had to read those plates pretty fast as they went by. Cars had plates on both the front and back bumpers, so that made it a little easier. We'd take turns adding up the numbers and letters as the cars sped past and whoever ended up with the best poker hand on his license plate won. We also played "foreign license plates", the key being to find a plate from another state. We rarely had a

"The Bench"
(left to right) Joe Conrad, Billy Rhodes, Oscar Burket, Charl McCoy,
Simon Weaver, Unknown

winner from any further than Virginia or maybe New York. Ohio and Maryland were pretty common, with anything west of the Mississippi a rare find.

There were times when the kids on the bench overflowed onto the concrete steps of Piney's, and Bertha would come out to scoot us off so the customers could get in and out of the beer joint and gas station.

Many baseball games were replayed on that old bench and I dare say some horse-trading was initiated there, too. It was told that this was the scene of some of the best horse-trading deals of that time, with Charlie

"The Bench" Early 1950's
(left to right) Henry Burket, Davey Walls, Gene Gonsman,
Paul Weaver, Hezzie Thompson, Eddie Miller

McCoy being one of the best traders around. Those who came to town to trade usually went home a little wiser, though rarely having gotten the better end of the deal.

From unwritten accounts of this part of local history, I learned that two of the qualities a horse-trader looked for were speed and durability. With this in mind, the traders would "show" their steeds by either racing down Newry

McCoy Brothers - Early 1900's

Road to Catfish Road, or down Newry Road to the Malone Bridge at Puzzletown.

According to my source on horse-trading lore, all one

4

McCoy's Tavern

could see on the day of the event was dust flying up from the dirt roads and sparks flying off the horses' shoes. Gospel truth...what an era, too soon forgotten!

Inside the beer parlor at McCoy's there was another large bench, my best guess it having been a former church pew. This bench was reserved for Warren "Piney" McCoy. One day, I may have been five or six, I climbed up on that bench with Piney, and as was his custom, he fell sound asleep...unfortunately, I happened to be right beside him, and soon, under him. Bertha, seeing my plight, roused Piney with a shout, "Warren, get up! You're gonna suffocate the boy!" He would've too, because when Piney slept, "all was right with the world" as they say.

Another incident that put fear in my heart came about one summer day when I was hanging out at McCoy's. (Now that I look back, it's no wonder that I was my mother's favorite...I was never home!) At that time, Father Edward Hickey was the pastor at St. Pat's and known to imbibe a bit in the "spirits". Piney's was one of his favorite watering holes.

Back in 1937 or '38, priests must have viewed owning a big car as prestigious, as they all had one. Father Hickey's was a large black Buick of some unknown make and model. As luck would have it, I was at Piney's one day after Father had been there for quite a while. He was known as a bit of a cut-up, and as he was leaving, he picked me up, put me on top of that big black Buick and pretended to pull away with me perched precariously on top. Someone told Bertha, who flew out of the tavern and yelled at Father, "If you don't get that boy down from there, I'll kill you!"

I reminded Bertha of this incident some years later, and while not denying it, she admitted that she really would have brought some "hurt" on the good Pastor!

I remember once my brother Jake and his friend Johnny McCoy decided to walk to Puzzletown to see their friends Joe and Charlie Moyer and took me with them. I was about five and I guess they would've been in their teens. It was mid-summer and scorching hot. We had made it to Sipes' farm before my short little legs gave out and I had to rest. The boys threatened to leave me by the side of the road if I didn't get up, so I cried... they ended up taking turns carrying me on their backs and eventually we made it to Moyer's. The return trip, thank goodness, was made in the back of Charlie Moyer's pickup truck.

The Moyer's would drive in to McCoy's Tavern most every Saturday night for a few "Old German's" and a bull session, with politics and new farming methods among the favorite topics chewed over back then.

I would go over to McCoy's when Joe and Charlie were there and we would play a game that they made up involving beer caps. In those days beer only came in bottles, and the used caps were kept in a can on the table. Underneath each cap was a cork insert that sealed the bottle in order to retain the freshness of the brew.

The game – before I got there, one of these rascals would pry out the cork insert and put a dime under it, then put the cork back in the cap. They would sit me down in front of a can full of beer caps and I would religiously pry the cork out of each one of those aluminum caps in search of a dime. They had evidently marked the cap, because as I unwittingly pried them open, one after another, Joe or Charlie would pick out the marked one, pry off the cap and exclaim, "Holy Smokies, there's another one!" I'm not sure how many years I fell for this fool game, but there was a good end result as I always went home with that dime.

It was about this time in my life that I acquired the distinctive nickname that defines me to this day. The time frame of 1936 or '40 being pre-television, our primary source of entertainment was the radio. Along with the weekly schedule of serials such as The Lone Ranger, The Green Hornet, Mr. Keene - Tracer of Lost Persons, and the one and only Tom Mix, there were some musical shows. Among them was the Saturday Night Barn Dance, broadcast live from Wheeling, West Virginia.

There was a hillbilly band called the "Hoosier Hot Shots" and the bandleader's name was Hezzikiah Abernathy. Hezzikiah had the dubious talent of having mastered the slide whistle in addition to many other instruments. As the band would warm up, someone would yell, "Are you ready, Hezzie?" and he would open up with this crazy sounding gadget.

Duly impressed, I saved up five- cents to send to the Ralston Cereal Company (along with a box top), and soon received my own bonafide whistle! After that, when the band yelled, "Are you ready, Hezzie?" and Hezzikiah pulled out his slide whistle, I would toot mine in time with that bandleader ... and the name has stuck all these years later. To this day I am still asked, "How in the world did you get that nickname?" and I have to explain.

"Are You Ready Hezzie?"
The Hoosier Hot Shots
on WLS Saturday Night Barn Dance

My girls tell me they can determine how long someone has known me by what they call me..."Hezzie" or "Frank".

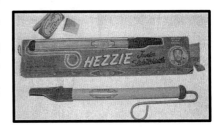

Speaking of nicknames, it seems that most small town guys back then had one. My dad's nickname was "Deadeye", as he lost an eye in the 1920's as a result of a railroad accident. Over the years, I've been at a function of some sort and run into someone who knew my dad and they'll say, "I bet you're one of Deadeye's boys." I've

NICKNAMES

Long John. . Leroy Moses	Zippy. . . . . C. Beigle
Scappy . . . . . . P. Weaver	Pank . . . . F. Weaver
Pepsi . . . . . . F. Gonsman	Bunk . . . . . . F. Gonsman
Tilly . . . . . . W. Thompson	Monk. . . . . D. Conrad
Pop. . . . . B. Sell	Gopher . . . . . . W. Hoover
W.O.. . . . . . . W.O. Wimer	Whitey . . . . . . W. Conrad
Humpy. . . . . . . M. Shaw	Whitey . . . . C. Wyant
Humpy. . . . . . . J. Beigle	Wash . . . . G. Weaver
Fezzi . . . . L. Leighty	Slim . . . . . . E. McFadden
Speed . . . . F. Burk	Coonie . . . . . . C. Conrad
Swampy . . . . . H. Benton	Jabbers . . Clifton Holland
Sickle . . . . R. Beigle	Bones . . . . George Claar
Shank . . . . C. Fissel	Capacity . . . . . P. Cassidy
Geichy. . . . . M. Shaw	Slugger . . . . . C. Cassidy
Doody. . . . H. Benton, Sr.	Sammy. . . . . . . D. Moses
Doc . . . Doc Montgomery	Jessy . . . . C. Conrad
Doc . . . . R. Gonsman	Scrawny . . . . . W. Conrad
Big Indian . . . . K. Berkey	Spit . . . . B. Shaw
Rabbit . . . . L. Smith	Daddy. . . . . J. Bogle
Peenie. . . . . K.Diehl	Peezy . . . . P. Imler
Piney. . . . . . . W. McCoy	Tappy . . . . G. Glass
Boogie . . . . J. Benton	Gus . . . . W. Black
Biggy Bo . . . . . . G. Bogle	Gandy . . . . C. Thompson
Ben Turpin . . . G. Conrad	Dizzy. . . . . . . Don Trexler
Red . . . . E. Fissel	Skip . . . . J. Beigle
Red . . . . R. Hite	Hezzie . . . . F. Thompson
Red . . . . K. Moses	Popeye. . . . P. Thompson
Taxi . . . . F. Conrad	Jake. . . . . . R. Thompson
Fat. . . . . R. Fissel	Dewey . . . . R. Thompson
Mutsie. . . . . . . R. Conrad	Butch . . . . . E. Thompson
Prig. . . . . F. Berkey	Babe . . . . . D. Thompson
Pope. . . . . C. Hite	Tater Diggle. . . . T. Beigle
Dinky . . . . P. Muri	Baseball Joe . . R. Conrad
Tarzan . . . . D. Burk	White Flash . . . J. McCoy

9

always dreaded hearing that, but it could've been worse...his other nickname was "Mouthy".

More than a few in our family had unusual nicknames – Jake, Popeye, Dewey, Butch, Babe and my sisters, Phitty or Turtle and Honey. My thanks to Glenn and Wayne Conrad for compiling the list of nicknames on the previous page.

Back then, there weren't too many families who had "inside" bathrooms and the Thompson's were no exception. Outhouses were usually located at the end of the yard, as far away from the house as possible, but still accessible on those cold winter nights. Our outhouse was at the end of a very long boardwalk. Every spring, depending on the size of your household and wintertime usage, the outhouse had to be moved and new retention holes dug — no concrete holding tanks back then!

One day, I was playing near the outhouse and forgot to stay clear of the previous location. Since warm weather had thawed the ground, I immediately went into that hole up to my knees and lost a shoe! Dutiful boy that I was, I informed my mother about what I had done, and she in turn, told my dad. I remember her telling me later that he wasn't as concerned with my welfare as he was to how I was going to "retrieve" that shoe. I imagine it's still at the bottom of the hole! This must not have been an unusual occurrence, as I was told my sister Phyllis did the same thing.

Being the frugal man he was, or maybe just due to the size of our family, my dad had decided that we could forgo the luxury of store-bought bathroom tissue, opting instead to have us use the "catalog" brand. In order to procure this item, my brothers would go downtown and solicit a variety of catalogues -- Sears and Roebuck, Montgomery Ward and various other mail order books.

It was later brought up that my dad preferred not to use the Spiegel pages, as they were too shiny!

The interior of our little outhouse was lined with cardboard boxes, which supposedly added some semblance of insulation for the occupant. We also employed the use of a variety of "two-holers" over the years, none of which I remember had many amenities. Enough said about this facet of our early lives, except that at some point we were able to afford store-bought tissue and glad of it!

Some of the old-timers will remember the existence of the town pump, located next to the Glass/Campbell house and across from McCoy's on the "Diamond". As near as can be determined, the pump was placed around 1884 and remained there until the 1940's. There was an old metal cup that hung on the pump and served as a communal drinking cup for anyone desiring a cold respite on a hot day. Looking back, I'm surprised the whole town didn't come down with a communicable disease from sharing that cup!

You'll notice the toll gate in the center of the photo of McMaster's Corner where, for a nickel, you were given access to our little town and its surroundings.

The Franklin House and the North end toll gate
on the Upper Diamond

McMaster's Store - 1876
Old town pump and water trough on lower left

ABOVE: Early parade watchers in front of Franklin Hotel, 1926. First row: Melvin Shaw, Rodney Conrad, John McCoy, Luke Smith, Bill Black. Second row: Earl McFadden, Nelson Conrad, Joe Conrad, Piney McCoy, Archie Lykens, Paul Weaver, Eddie Miller, Walter Thompson, Keith Dugan, Irvin Eicher, Don Weaver, Sam Moses, Edwin Wertz, Rule Conrad. Third row: Elmer Helsel, Wilford Fickes Black, Dalton Black. Background: Fat Fissel.

RIGHT: Joe and Lou Diehl, North end toll gate keepers

BELOW: Bedford Street, South end toll gate

Montgomery's Service Station (The location of the old Wonder Bar)

Vehicles shown are 1924 & 1929 Ford

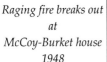

Raging fire breaks out at McCoy-Burket house 1948

Newry could also boast of a few barbershops at various times, one of them Mr. Glunt's, which was located in a small storeroom at the end of the Montgomery building and down the street from the Wonder Bar. Later, a barbershop occupied the corner room of George Campbell's house on the Diamond.

Our neighbor, Eddie Cassidy, was the family barber and I recall his haircuts not being the most pleasant experience for a young child. His scissors were always dull and he'd yell if we moved around in the makeshift barber seat. This consisted of an old kitchen chair with two or three Sears and Roebuck or Montgomery Ward catalogues piled high to get us little ones up to his level. Haircuts back then were five cents, but with inflation, went up to ten! A haircut for ten cents - those were the days!

Mr. Trexler, known as "Pappy" to us kids, was another local barber and also a janitor at St. Pat's. I'm not sure that he actually had a barber's license or was just self-taught, but he kept his barbering tools in a closet at the new St. Pat's. One day Jim Stalter and I got into Pappy's tools and Jim said that if I let him cut my hair, he would let me cut his. I soon found out Jim was no barber! He butchered my hair and then took off for home...needless to say, our friendship was strained for the rest of the summer, and I'm sure my mother was not too pleased either!

Bill Hite told me once that Pappy Trexler, being short and wiry, could do a trick where he would leap with both feet into a three foot high barrel or tub, and in the same movement, jump out again!

In the mid 1930's, our family moved from Newry to a large house halfway between Newry and Catfish. Mr. Rath owned the property at the time and the rent back then was fifteen dollars a month. Imagine!

Early memories of the house are of a large kitchen, along with an "out kitchen" where Mom washed clothes, a dining room, living room, a large hall with stairs to the second floor and a parlor. The parlor was where the good furniture was kept and off-limits except when "company" came. The curved stairwell was located off the dining

Catfish House

room, but ours didn't lead to the servant's quarters like those in the fancy houses!

Like our Newry house, our bathroom was situated about 100' to the northwest and had the same amenities, or lack thereof, as our previous ones.

My sister Phyllis tells me that our brother Paul was born while we were living there, weighing in at about four pounds and so small that he slept in a dresser drawer for the first four months. Anyone familiar with Paul knows that he hasn't stopped growing since! He was born with a webbed hand, which allowed for much speculation at our house..."Maybe he's gonna be a duck!" I remember our neighbors asking if he could swim when he was born! A side note – out of all twelve kids, Paul was the only one born in a hospital!

Our sister Audrey had moved out by then, having married Joe Hofer from the Juniata section of Altoona. Joe worked for Western Union at the time delivering telegrams on his bicycle and would ride it all the way to Newry to visit her. I remember thinking that he sure must have loved her to do that!

Joe & Audrey Hofer 1937

Brother Ray spent some of his early summers at Uncle Cloyd and Aunt Lilly's home in Altoona, and would return

Raymond, 1931

when school began. As they didn't have any children, they tended to spoil Ray a bit, although I'm not sure he would admit to that!

So, in addition to our parents, Jake, Ray, Phyllis, Paul, Joe, Jim, Dewey, and Butch and I lived in this big house.

When you look at those numbers, you have to wonder where everyone slept! There were four or five bedrooms on the second floor and two or three boys would share a room. Each room had a big metal bed with open metal springs covered with a straw or "tic" mattress. The mattress was made out of a material similar to a flour sack, large enough to cover a bed and had a pocket to hold the straw as the bedding. Every couple of months, Jake and Ray would take these mattresses over to Pap Hite's, where for a quarter, they would refill them. I remember that when Paul and I got older, we fell heir to this task.

This house provided a great form of "entertainment" for my brothers and me. Off of one of the bedrooms was an unfinished attic or loft that in cold weather was occupied by families of field mice. We couldn't let an opportunity to hone our shooting skills pass by, so it became our own personal shooting range. We brought out our Red Ryder BB gun and took turns taking potshots at those little critters! I don't recall how long it took our dad to catch on to our sport before he sealed up the entrance holes, but it was great fun while it lasted!

Our Catfish house had a pipeless coal furnace and our "central heating" was an open iron grate located between the living room and kitchen. For sure this was the most utilized space on those cold winter mornings, as there was no heat in our bedrooms, just a hole in the floor covered by another grate!

The basement had a dirt floor with a spring running through it, originating from a stream behind our neighbors, the Cooper's. It was well below ground and the water was always cold. As our method of refrigeration at the time was an icebox, we utilized this spring for meats and other perishable items.

Ralph "Pap" Hite's farm was our source for milk and some of our meat. The farm was located about a half-mile from our house, through the fields, and we took turns hiking for milk. I don't know how many jugs a day we went through, but I'm sure our family kept a couple of cows pretty busy! I could fill many more pages just with memories of all of us growing up in this house.

I realize that I haven't mentioned in my writings thus far that our family never owned a car, so our main mode of transportation was "foot power." My dad rode a work bus to and from the PRR shops, and as we got older we would walk into Newry, about one and a half miles, and hitch-hike to our destination. In those days, you could trust a person to pick you up and the fare was always just a hearty "thank you".

Living out in the country, we were accustomed to

home delivery by various vendors. Our breadman worked for Livingston Bakery and was a nice old gent who on occasion treated us with samples. Samples were outdated cupcakes and pies that couldn't be sold, so rather than throw them out, he gave them to us. I dare say our family was one of this guy's best customers and probably one of the few who paid on time, considering we were in the throes of the "Big Depression".

Another home deliveryman was Mr. Campbell, the McNess man, who sold medicine out of a big black leather bag. God only knows what all he had in that bag, but that's where the Sloan's liniment, Doan's pills, analgesic balm, Cloverine salve, and many other remedies came from that stocked our family's medicine cabinet. We also had the Watkin's man, the McNess guy's competition, and he also sold our family some "cure-alls".

Most reliable was a potion named "Father John's Medicine" a mix of cod liver oil and other ingredients. Although sold as a cough medicine, this licorice-tasting syrup was usually given to every kid in the family on their way out the door to school in the morning (from the same spoon!) Due to this magic elixir, or maybe in spite of it, we rarely needed a doctor's visit.

Lee Dodson

Most families back then had an iceman, ours being Lee Dodson from East Freedom. We attended St. Pat's with his children –

Loretta, Conwell, Ray, Colleen and probably a couple more whose names escape me. Brother Paul and I always met Mr. Dodson on his stop at our house and would gobble up the ice chips that came off of those twenty-five and fifty- pound blocks.

My recollection of these next gentlemen is slim, but they were certainly some of the more interesting characters from my early years, the junk man in particular. He would make his rounds shouting his sales pitch, "Rags, bones and old iron!" That phrase still puzzles me, as rags and iron I can understand, but bones? I do know this, if he got rags from our house, they were just that, as our seven or eight boys at the time usually wore their clothes until they weren't fit for anything but rags.

Another visitor who made periodic stops was the fellow who sharpened tools, knives, scissors, scythes, clippers and anything else with a blade. I'm not sure of the fee for this service, but likely it was minimal.

Back then I didn't know what "The Depression" meant, or even the fact that we were in one. I guess my mother and father just made sure that we all had enough food to eat — we didn't think about where it came from. I'm sure that our family, like others, ate our share of small and large game. It was said that Newry guys were reportedly some of the best shots in the county. The following photos will attest to that fact.

BIG SHOTS

Fat Glunt, Ferdy Hite
Panky Weaver, Pat George in 1936

Loris Glunt, Ferdy Hite
Pat George in 1937

Panky Weaver,
Kenny Berkey,
Ted Smith,
Quentin Berkey,
Peany Diehl

Geichey Shaw and Rodney Conrad
1936

*Sharply dressed
Ted Long, Wilse Benton,
Jack Spidle at Bell Camp,
Karthas 1942*

Newry Deer Hunters 1937 – First row-Bill Imler, Wilford Black, Pat George, Jack Spidle, Rodney Conrad, Jessie Conrad, Bill Cooper. Second row-Gerald Moses, Pat Wilt, Bob Leighty, Harry Benton, Gerald Gonsman, Leo Lanzendorfer, Francis Bleicher, Francis Weaver, Paul Weaver, Pat Diehl. Third row-Herb Cassidy, Maxwell Conrad, Dave Leighty, Donald Weaver, Elmer Glass, Clarence Niswonger, Paul Leighty. Petroleum Line, east of Puzzletown.

*Yeager Farm 1930s-
Walter Thompson
Rhuel Conrad,
Bill Conrad,
Wilford Black,
Paul Leighty,
Charles Conrad,
Pat Diehl
and Panky Weaver.*

Our house, among many in the country, was well marked as a stop for bums, or hobos, as we knew them. They probably guessed by the sound of so many kids running around that they could get a sandwich made with Mom's homemade bread and a good cup of coffee or a cold drink.

Back then, a "mark" was strategically placed on a tree or telephone pole by the roadside or on a house or fencepost by one or more of these fellows, indicating whether a house was friendly or not. The history of these men tells a lot and defines the era in many ways. The adjacent page shows some of the various marks left by hobos to let others know if it was a worthwhile stop.

In 1933, Franklin D. Roosevelt started the National Recovery Act, or NRA. This was a program designed to help the unemployed, there being many in those unfortunate circumstances. Other programs included the Works Progress Administration or WPA, and the Civilian Conservation Corp or CCC.

WPA provided employment for older men. They worked road construction and helped build many of the stone culverts and bridges along our highways that still exist today (it was nicknamed the "We Poke Along" program, as the workers could often be seen leaning on their shovels or lounging along the roadside). The CCC program provided employment for the younger guys and was operated like a camp. One of my local historians, Glenn Conrad, tells me that Dick Moses, a boy from Newry, went to this camp. It was located in Trough Creek in Huntingdon County and exists today

Key to Hobo /TrampSigns

1. Main Street good for begging
2. Rock Pile in connection with Jail
3. Saloons in Town
4. Prohibitionin Town
5. Police are Hostile, look out
6. Police not Hostile to Tramps
7. Police Hostile to Tramps
8. Leaving Railroad for Highway or across country
9. Railroad Police not Hostile
10. Railroad Police Hostile
11. Used in connection with any other sign means next turn
12. Church or Religious People
13. Town is Hostile - Get out quick
14. Main Street N.G.
15. Good People Live Here
16. Cranky Woman or Dog
17. People do not give
18. Bad Man lives here
19. Negro section good for Hoboes
20. Cooties in Jail
21. Good clean Jail
22. Jail good but prisoners starve
23. Jail filthy
24. City Police are in Plain Clothes
25. Workhouse in connection with Jail
26. Waiting in Town for Person Named
27. Circle Town
28. Jail good for night's Lodging

as a Pennsylvania State Park. A couple of the older guys from hunting camps on Diamond Valley Road in Petersburg, where I'm a member of the Leading Ridge Camp, tell me that there is still much of the young men's craftsmanship visible in the stone and log camps on the state forest roads.

Included in the NRA was a program where women sewed clothing for young people. My sister Phyllis remembers wearing skirts, fashioned from old flour and feed sacks, embossed patterns and all. Boys shirts and girls blouses were made of similar material. She also recalls being given an outfit made of gray or brown denim and a white blouse with a Peter Pan collar to go with it. In those days it wasn't hard to distinguish the poor kids, as we all had the "uniform" look. Pride was lost in the reality of having good clean clothing to wear to school.

I'm sure many alive today are grateful for the programs that provided a little extra income to keep families like ours clothed and fed.

The property we lived on at this time had an old frame garage, a barn of sorts. This structure had many functions, as we stored coal and wood for our heat along with my dad using it to raise chickens for the family. Dad was pretty adept at chicken farming and used a brooding pen for "peeps". When the weather turned cold, we kept this low slung, metal cage in the kitchen to keep the eggs warm until they hatched, along with straw and an electric globe light to provide heat.

Early one morning Mom got up to get her brood off to their various destinations and entered the kitchen only to be greeted by an enormous rat that had gained entry into the peep cage. She let out a blood curdling scream and headed for the nearest chair! I'm sure one of us boys quickly came to her rescue and removed the offender.

The barn also served as a clubhouse for the boys and girls in the neighborhood. Phyllis and her friends spent many hours playing with their cut-out dolls, assembled from paper ones taken from the Sunday newspaper. I remember one of them was named "Tillie the Toiler", a name that always struck me as being odd. Tillie had little outfits that fit over her body and the girls took great pride in their collection of dolls.

In this era of pre-television, the newspaper was a real treat for us and we looked forward to reading "the funnies" and the sports pages.

The chickens Dad raised were primarily for food, so we bought eggs from Mrs. Cooper, a kindly, older neighbor lady whose husband passed away before we moved into the neighborhood. The Cooper boys were good friends of my brothers Jake and Ray, as they were older than Paul and I. Bill, Pat, Tom and Jack were fun neighbors and I remember Ray and Jack could be counted on to cause a little commotion from time to time.

They both had BB guns, probably Red Ryders, and occasionally Ray and Jack would have a gun battle — one using the outhouse as a fort and the other commandeering the barn. God must have been watching over these two because somehow neither lost an eye in battle, though I'm sure many a rear-end was stung when retreat was sounded!

Paul and I eventually took to this game, with one of our shooting partners being Carl "Whitey" Wyant. Carl, his sister Mary Catherine, and their mom and dad lived up the road from us. Bob and Mickey Rentz lived in the house between us and had a pretty daughter, Joyce Ann, who was slightly younger than I was. It's funny how looking back, there didn't seem to be any ugly girls in Newry!

Mary Catherine and Joyce Ann were two of Phyllis' friends, and Mary Catherine and I were in the same class at St. Pat's. As I wasn't too smart, I used to talk her into "helping" me with my homework.

Phyllis tells of the time she and Mary Catherine were playing near the Newry Creek when it was at its spring height. Mary Catherine fell in, so Phyllis jumped in after her and dragged her out. To this day Mary Catherine thanks Phyllis for saving her life.

Since Paul and I were pretty close in age, we were pals and always together. My recollections of brothers Joe, Jim, Dewey and Butch during those years in the late 1930's aren't as strong, but I know they all had their special friends.

Whitey, Paul and I, being about the same age, would play together – marbles being one of our favorite games. Whitey was pretty good, but my brother Ray was most likely the best "shooter" around. On occasion us little guys would get to play the "big ring", but usually only the best shooters played there.

In the game of marbles, the outside ring measured about eight feet in diameter with the marbles (a number predetermined by the number of shooters) placed in a smaller ring, about two feet in diameter. The object was to use a large marble (a shooter) to try to knock the other guy's marbles out of the ring. You kept on shooting if you scored. The rules were "knuckles down tight, no hunchin', no innies and no steelies unless all players were allowed to use them". A steelie was a steel ball bearing of various sizes that gave the shooter a distinct advantage over the other shooters. Steelies were usually procured from a relative who worked on the railroad or in a factory that used ball bearings.

Needless to say, brother Ray usually ended up with everyone's marbles.

I know that on more than one occasion we got "physical" as a result of this game. When Whitey and I were about seven or eight years old, we got into one of our more serious scuffles. All I can recall is that for some reason, in the middle of a game, he grabbed up his marbles and took off for home. His house was about two blocks up the road and I didn't catch him until he was at his back door. Unfortunately, his mother saw me chasing him and came after me with a broom. To this day when I see his sister, Mary Catherine, I remind her of how her mother gave me a good beating.

Of course, Mary Catherine tells a different version of the story. She said that she, Phyllis and I were playing and I did something to make her mad, so she beat me up. She said my mother came flying out of the back door and whacked her with a broom as I lay helpless on the ground. It sounds unusual for Mom, all of 4'11" to be violent, but that was her unwritten law, "Don't mess with my boys!"

One of the neighbors not too fond of the Thompson boys was Sam Maurer, who lived next door to Wyant's and was the proud owner of a grape vineyard with the largest, sweetest purple grapes you've ever seen. I recall more than a few trips by us boys to sample these beauties...unbeknownst to Sam!

Sam also had a peach orchard on his property that bore some of the finest peaches in the area, along with a cherry orchard consisting of big oxheart cherries that again tempted us kids to "test" the crop on occasion.

Sam had a brother, Howard who was mentally challenged, and for some reason Whitey, Paul and I used to tease him...God forgive us now.

Sam's grape vineyard was located on either side of his house and to the rear of the property. One day Whitey, Paul and I were sneaking through the vineyard to test the grapes for quality and Howard came tearing out of the house with some kind of gun, a .22 or a shotgun. With Howard's mental capacity and us not knowing his shooting abilities, we quickly dropped to a prone position and hid in the grass. I'm not sure how long we laid there, but we thought we were goners!

Sam had sort of a whippoorwill farm and a large bank barn that housed his grain and hay crops along with two big 'ole mules, Harry and Bess. It didn't take long to discover that these mules didn't much care for me.

The open corral surrounding the barn had a five-foot stockade fence, and one day while riding my little bike past, I noticed the gate was open, so I closed it and went on my way. Pedaling down the road, I heard the distinct sound of hooves coming from behind. Looking back, I saw Harry and Bess lumbering down the road right at me!

Well, I jumped off my bike, threw it aside and ran as fast as I could through the Shaw sisters' yard. Edith and Grace Shaw were single ladies, both school teachers, who lived in their family home after their parents passed away. They witnessed the whole scene, and quickly snatched me up onto their front porch. Old Harry and Bess headed back down the road and the lovely ladies calmed my fears with cookies and a cold drink until I settled down.

I don't know how long those ornery mules lived, but I made sure to steer clear of them from then on!

Speaking of orchards, evidently the Newry area at the time held some fame as a peach growing industry of sorts. Other orchards of note were located on Jim Harker's property south of Newry and one operated by Francis "Panky" Weaver (my friend Scrappy's brother) and Dave Leighty. This last orchard was located up by the Malone Bridge in Puzzletown on what was commonly known as the old Weaver tract. John Wyant also had a great orchard with peaches and apples, and Benton's orchard was up the hill behind the Cooper's property.

I won't admit to having "visited" all these orchards, but I do remember enjoying a variety of fresh, juicy fruit back then!

The picture below shows some of the local boys taking time off from apple pickin' to mug for the camera at Benton's Orchard. It was said that the guns were used to ward off bears! What a priceless photo, and one I'm glad I came across to include in this journal!

Jack Spindle, George Benton, Jim Malone,
Harry Benton, Bill Cooper at Benton's Orchard 1939

One family who lived close to us was Sheldon Hite's. Several of the Hite girls went to St. Pat's with us and had to walk about a quarter to a half a mile farther than our house to get to school. Delores was probably Ray's age, Jane Frances and Marjorie were within a year or so of my age, and Lois was Paul's age. There were also several younger kids.

Marjorie and I share the following story — back then our mothers purchased some of our clothing from a catalog, either Sears and Roebuck's or Montgomery Ward. When Marjorie and I were in second grade, our mothers both ordered snowsuits for us, the one or two-piece kind with elastic wrist and ankle bands.

In time, the snowsuits arrived at our respective homes. Unbeknownst to us or our mothers, they were exact in both style and color. Sure enough, Marj and I met on the road to school, having picked the same day to show off our new outerwear. Imagine my surprise — there she was with "my" snowsuit on! Of course, Marj greeted me with a shout, "Hezzie's wearing a girl's snowsuit!"

It was a long, long time till I lived that down! The story haunts me to this day, as Marj never failed to tell it as often as possible!

Another incident that occurred on the way to school involved my buddy Whitey and I. We were walking down the road by the Sell's house and noticed a skunk crawling into an iron pipe that ran under the road. Not for us to leave well enough alone, we decided to tease Mr. Skunk until he did what most skunks do in that situation and "unloaded" on us! Although we smelled to high heaven, we knew we couldn't be late for Mass, so we hurried along to St. Pat's. Having made it through, we thought we were home free until Sister Mary Jean, having a nun's keen sense of smell, strongly suggested Whitey and I return home and change, which we did – and vowed never to challenge a skunk again!

Brother Paul reminded me of several events that occurred in his early years. As he tells it, he was four or five when he attempted to help Mom run clothes through our old wringer-type washing machine and somehow inserted his arm into the wringer along with a piece of clothing. It drew his arm in up to his shoulder and continued to grind and wring. He says he was able to get Mom's attention and she yanked him out fast. He still has the scars to show for it.

I don't know what made Paul think he could operate a wringer washer and believe it or not, my brother Butch pulled the same stunt years later with the same results...my poor mother!

Paul also tells of the time he and I went fishing at Pap Hite's creek (which is pronounced "crick" as I'm sure most of you know!) As we were walking through the field toward the creek, I was showing Paul how I was going to cast and catch "the big one". (I guess I haven't changed much!) As I cast over my head, Paul got in the way of the fishing line and the hook caught him right in the nose! Needless to say, he didn't wait for me to extract the hook and instead took off running for home, about a quarter of a mile.

Grandpap Leonard, my mom's father, was visiting at the time and Paul, with line and hook and blood flying, ran screaming into the yard, where Grandpap met him. We figured he would somehow "surgically" remove it, and he did — he grabbed that hook at the point of entry and yanked it out — no anesthesia, gauze or stitches given. Mom probably just doused the wound with good old peroxide.

Of course, no apology would suffice, and I remember getting into big trouble for not being more careful!

A more serious accident involving Paul and I took

place at Pap Hite's farm while Ferdinand Hite, Pap's son, was plowing one of the lower fields. It was early spring and a great time to pick nightcrawlers, especially out of a newly plowed field. Ferdy had warned us to stay away from the plow and keep our hands back, as when he came to the end of each row, he would manually raise and lower the plow. Of course Paul, who always seemed to want to "test" things, reached down to pick a worm just as Ferdy lowered that plow, and it lopped half his middle finger off. He took off for home, running like a bat out of hell, while I stopped long enough to pick up the finger. By the time I made it home, Mom was already making arrangements with a neighbor to take Paul to Nason Hospital. I went along and rode in the back of their pickup truck, holding on to that bloody finger all the way, I guess in the hope that the doctor could sew it back on. He couldn't, and the finger ended up being thrown away, which really upset me because I wanted it — don't ask me why!

Living along Catfish Road offered our gang of boys a lot of opportunities to get into trouble. One day Ray and several boys were playing in "the swamp," a field next to our house that had a spring running through it. This incident must have taken place in mid-summer because the ground at the time was really dry. Somehow Ray managed to set the field on fire, but luckily the breadman and some neighbors happened to be nearby and they all ran to extinguish it before it got out of control.

I'm sure the next hot thing we witnessed was my dad's breath when he reamed Ray out!

Homemade Fun

The go-cart pictured above was hand made by the father of Lee Lanzendorfer, Leo, who was the driver of the cart. The cart pulled a wagon that held two students traveling from home to St. Patrick's Catholic School in Newry, 3.5 miles from Puzzletown. The go-cart was made from junk. Wheels were cut from logs and the outside diameter was covered with old tire tread fastened with nails. The go-cart made the school run for about six to eight weeks before the Pennsylvania State Police caught on and stopped them.

Entertainment in those days was just what you made it. A few of the games we played were "kick the can" and "tag", a game with rules that seemed to change daily and at times had boundaries extending far into the woods behind our houses. "Capture the flag" was a great game that required little skill, but lots of sneaking ability. A ball game I remember was "Rolly, rolly over," where teams would gather on either side of a house and someone from one team would throw a ball over the roof and yell "rolly, rolly over!" After the other team caught it, they would run around to chase and try to hit the opposing players with the ball. Can you imagine kids today playing a game like this? No batteries needed for our games back then, just a lot of imagination!

While not a "game" per se, I can remember taking White House milk cans and stomping them in the middle so they would wrap around my shoes. They made a sound like a horse clattering up the old macadam road — a sure way to pull the soles and heels off of your (most likely) one and only pair of shoes!

An event we kids always hung around to watch took place during the annual butchering season. When the hogs were ready to butcher, a crew of men adept at this task would meet in the slaughter shop, next to the milk house on Pap Hite's farm. A hog would be brought in and felled with a well-placed shot to the head, then immersed in a large vat-type tank filled with scalding hot water, which evidently softened the skin. It was then raised by means of a pulley and chain device to allow the men to remove all the hair on the hog with large wire brushes, after which they would skin it.

Boys being boys, we enjoyed the whole process, our favorite being the rendering. Without getting too graphic, rendering was accomplished by placing a variety of hog parts, including the skin, in a large cylindrical press. With pressure applied, liquid "lard" would come out the bottom drain.

The product that remained was pressed into a round, twelve-inch by four-inch cake, called "cracklins" — a delicacy worth fighting over. Judging by today's health standards, I'm sure each cake contained enough cholesterol and fat to last a lifetime!

My cousin Ruth Thompson, now deceased, told me that once, while working at Leighty's Farm Market, she took her whole day's pay (twenty-five cents), bought a cake of cracklins and ate the entire thing by herself...she also shared that she "paid the price" the next day for eating that greasy treat!

Another by-product of hog butchering was "pig souse", a gelatin-type mixture consisting of meat from the pig's feet. The feet meat was mixed with vinegar and the broth that was obtained from cooking various other parts of the pig, including the skin and ligaments. This mixture was cooked along with fresh pork, placed in an oblong metal pan and put in the cooler. Another delicacy supplied by the neighborhood butcher.

In those days, meat was considered a commodity and farmers didn't waste much...it was said that all was used but the "oink"!

Ruth and I also reminisced about some of the other food we ate back then, like milk soup, coffee soup and gravy bread. A short description of milk or coffee soup — it consisted of several slices of our mother's homemade bread covered with either beverage according to your taste, or more likely, what was available. Gravy bread was the same – Mom's bread with her homemade gravy poured over the slices. These were pretty standard breakfasts and lunches back then, and while not fancy, were filling.

My sister Phyllis tells me that "poor" kids in school were given a bowl of mush for lunch made from corn meal, topped with honey or milk, a handful of walnuts and a cod liver oil capsule to keep from getting rickets. She also recalls a health nurse coming to visit periodically.

A big event in our youth was when Mr. Hamil, the County Agent, would come to Sam Maurer's farm to dynamite a ditch in one or more of the lower fields, which were frequently flooded. Evidently, the purpose was to divert the water into Poplar Run. I guess this solution worked, because those swampy fields then became tillable. A gang of us boys would gather to witness this spectacle and enjoyed every minute of it. Although I wasn't quite sure what all a County Agent did, I knew I would have liked that job!

Paul Burk, Piney Glass, Blair Sell, Harvey Sell,
Gerald Moses, Regis Stormer. Globe Run, 1925

As country kids, we used to get a kick out of seeing Bob "Harvey" Sell run his threshing machine past our house on the way to a threshing job. I never knew the intricacies of that machine, but it sure made a lot of racket!

We got used to seeing Harvey's brother, another elderly farmer, on the road in front of our house. He had a wagon pulled by a team of horses and drove past almost daily. Where he got his nickname is beyond me, but he was known as "Booper" Sell. Again, it goes to show that if you lived in Newry, you most likely had a nickname!

Jim and Ellen Smith lived beyond Mr. Sell's house. They were elderly and we never got to know them very well. When Paul and I were old enough to go to Newry to meet friends, we would have to pass their house to go to town. The Smith's had a large barn located close to the road and in that barn were two of the most ferocious dogs we had ever come across! Paul and I always had to sneak past, as those dogs had the keenest sense of hearing and invariably would attack the wooden barn doors as soon as we passed in front of them. All we'd see as we were running past was teeth — big teeth! I don't even want to think about what would've happened if those devil dogs had ever got a hold of us, but it probably would have added another interesting story for my journal!

Next to the Smith's house lived the Gonsman family, all seventeen of them! Eugene "Bunk" Gonsman was about Ray's age and they spent a lot of time together. The rest of the kids were older, except Mary Alice, another pretty Newry girl who was close to my age. I'm not sure where Mrs. Gonsman found the space, but she set up a room in their house that held a lending library, I believe part of an NRA project. We were allowed to sign out one book at a time, although I don't recall reading having been one of my favorite pastimes at that stage of my life!

Tragically, one of the saddest memories from my childhood involved Bussy Gonsman. In the early spring, Poplar Run rose up to four to six feet in depth due to the melting snow, and in April 1943, it was high. Bussy was seven or eight at the time and was watching the raging water with his sister, Denise, from the footbridge that crossed over Poplar Run on Pap Hite's farm. Somehow he lost his balance and fell into the stream. Denise tried

Elizabeth Rhodes, Poplar Run footbridge

valiantly to save him, but was unable to reach him, so she ran to get help. Soon word passed all over town and fire departments and volunteers came together to search the stream. Later that day, I believe it was Pat Kelly who found the small body lodged under a submerged tree. The whole town was devastated and the tragedy was not soon forgotten. Our hearts and prayers went out to the Gonsman family for their terrible loss.

Another project in the NRA was the summer playground program run by a gentleman by the name of Russell Clapper. I remember Mr. Clapper teaching us a good deal about organized sports, along with other fun activities.

Pet Show 1939. First ow-Paul Thompson, Joe Hite, Betty Beigle, Francis Cassidy. Second row-Pat Cassidy, Pat Kelly, Paul Muri, Roger Glass, John Stormer. Third row-Gladys Kelly, Marie Muri, Rita Hite, R.V. Cassidy, M. Alice Gonsman. Fourth row-Phitty Thompson, M.G. Boyer, Virgie Wilt, Charles Wilt, A. Boyer, Eugene Gonsman. Betty McCoy and Marion Shaw were on the ponies.

One of the annual events was the "Pet Show", which was open to all kids and their pets. As evidenced by this photo, quite a variety of entries were represented. My sister Phyllis entered a turtle or two, as she had developed the unusual habit of bringing home turtles from Pap Hite's and Duck Creek! She had big turtles and little baby

Phyllis and Mom 1950

turtles and kept them in our enclosed rear porch in tubs

and boxes. Sometimes she just let them run loose, which didn't please my dad. For some reason, he didn't like "tortles" as he called them, and I'm sure helped many escape over time. Phyllis was so well known for this pet project she ended up with the nickname "Turtle". The name followed her into nurses training in the late forties, and most of her fellow nurses and some family and friends still call her that.

A natural disaster spoken about often by the townspeople was the St. Patrick's Day Flood of 1936. From all accounts, it was a tragedy for residents and animals alike. It was told that there were buildings and animals floating down Poplar Run from Puzzletown and Phyllis remembers little pigs being swept into the torrential current. At the time she belonged to a 4H Club that had meetings at the Gonsman house, with members being mostly farm boys and girls.

It always puzzled me as to why God would send a flood to our little town on this particular day.

Mentioning the streams that ran through Pap Hite's farm brings to mind some of my brothers' and my fishing expeditions in the plentiful waters surrounding our home. Duck Creek was located near Bleicher's house and had its origin from a spring behind Shaw's Meat Market. It ran diagonally through Newry and joined Poplar Run near the lower section of Pap Hite's farm. Every spring, this stream became a spawning ground for "suckers." Suckers, for want of a better name, were very boney fish and utilized the muskrat holes and weeded overhangs in the stream to spawn. Few families used them as table fare. There was one gentleman, whose name escapes me, who nonetheless enjoyed them and would pay Jake fifty cents a half-bushel for his catch.

Jake and Ray were experts in the "handfeeling" method of fishing. This system required the fisherman to reach into the water while lying on his stomach, locate a fish with his hands and then clasp it tight and throw the fish up onto the bank. Handfeeling produced many a large fish for those who were not afraid to attempt this primitive method.

Paul and I also adopted this technique and eventually became somewhat proficient at catching the slippery natives to that stream. We also acquired another fishing skill we called "snaring", using a wooden pole with a noose made of copper wire attached to the end of it. Snaring was accomplished by maneuvering the noose over the fish's head while it was lying at the bottom of the stream, trying not to disturb it. If the fisherman was lucky enough to achieve this, he then jerked the noose tight and yanked the fish out of the water. The copper wire was usually procured from an old armature off of a tractor or other farm implement, but "borrowed" PRR wire worked best and was relatively easy to come by, if you know what I mean.

I taught Bill Hite this method and we both became experts. One time we were snaring and I caught an 18-inch "spottie", another type of fish that inhabited Poplar Run and had the shape of a sucker but with spots on its back. The scientific names for these fish weren't of any importance to us back then, so if they weren't suckers, they were spotties.

Bill Hite, 1944

I mention this particular incident because an 18-incher was a rare catch, and as Bill and I waded upstream for home with the spottie on a makeshift stringer, it somehow got loose, never to be seen again! I never forgave Bill for letting that huge fish get away, but even now he tells me that it wasn't his fault. That was over sixty years ago, and I'm still a little mad at him, because without the fish I wasn't able to brag to the locals about the "monster" I caught that day!

In the early 1940's, I had a friend named "Peanuts" Billotte who lived in the upper end of town with his family. We became good friends in school and enjoyed hanging out together.

One spring, just about the time that the Newry creek was flowing at its pre-flood stage, Peanuts and I decided to build a wood raft and float from the Rocks at Leighty's to Pap Hite's farm. We managed to scrounge up some old lumber and set to building the craft that would take us on our maiden voyage. I don't recall the 'size or method of construction of this raft, but we were able to finish it and carry it the two blocks to the creek, where we boarded and started downstream.

The next thing I remember was coming up from under the raft beside Peanut, both of us choking and gasping and clawing our way back to shore, two ten year olds, soaked to the skin with our hopes dashed.

We never did see our raft after that day. I suppose it crashed into bits and pieces downstream.

I don't believe either of us ever told anyone about our little expedition...for obvious reasons.

I should tell you that "Peanuts" was not his christened name, that being Cletus. When I questioned the origin of his nickname, he told me that a gentleman in Newry, one "Humpy" Beigle, bestowed it on him. Mr. Beigle said Clete was about as big as a peanut. He was about 5'2" stretched out, so the name was fitting.

Another favorite fishing spot we frequented was the "Long Hole", a swamp-like area down by St. Bernadine's Monastery in Kladder. It was quite a walk for us, but the resulting catch was always worth it. The locals said that there were pike in those waters four feet long! At the time I was probably all of four feet tall myself and had visions of pulling a fish out of that hole as big as me! It never happened, but I had fun trying. We did catch some small pike and lots of suckers.

The Long Hole was known as a breeding place for snapping turtles, and again, the locals told of snapping turtles as "big as a washtub" with mouths strong enough to bite a six-inch piece of willow in half. I remember thinking about that, and was always careful not to go in the water!

It was said the larger snapper turtles provided some pretty good meals, as the meat derived from the turtle was said purported to be better than steak. Having never tried this tasty fare, I cannot attest to its goodness. Rattlesnake meat was another delicacy the old guys loved, and I took them at their word on that, too!

This hole also produced large carp, known to most as a "trash" fish. Two older local women, Oletha Fissel and her mother, Bessie Hite apparently disagreed and were often seen throwing in their lines along the banks in pursuit of this fish. Oletha became brother Ray's mother-in-law later in life. She was a

Kladder Bridge

registered nurse and enjoyed spending her off-days fishing, either the river or at Saxton where the big ones grew. Carp were called "mud suckers" and had a muddy taste, but supposedly Mrs. Fissell prepared them in a fashion that they were tolerable.

Along with fish, chicken was a staple of our diet back then. As I've mentioned before, living in the country everybody had a chicken coop — most likely a wooden shack built up off the ground so coons, possums, skunks and other varmints couldn't get to the poultry. Coops were usually covered with tarpaper.

By this time my dad had gotten tired of raising chickens and sharing the peeps with the rats, so it was more convenient for him to go to the "sale" at

Showalter's Sale Barn and buy half a dozen chickens than raise them.

Seeing that we weren't using our coop, my "pyromaniac" brothers somehow convinced my dad to let them burn down the chicken coop…and therein lies the next tale.

It was a grand occasion and kids from all around came to watch as this stinking edifice burned to the ground, the tarpaper belching putrid smoke over the whole neighborhood.

As the fire subsided into a huge pile of hot, tarry goo, the boys became a daring group and challenged each other to jump over this mixture having a probable temperature in the hundreds of degrees. We all took turns and were successful until Karl "Red" Moses, a slim kid with long legs, took his turn. He either overestimated his stride or tripped, because he went flailing into this inferno and came out the other side screaming like a banshee Indian!

Karl took off through the swamp, literally a smoking, flaming ball of fire, with most of the spectators following him in "hot" pursuit, no pun intended. They were finally able to catch him and get him on the ground where they put him out. Someone ended up taking him to the hospital, where poor Red spent months in rehabilitation. It was a terrible accident and I'm sure he regretted his decision to participate in our little game.

I don't believe we burned any more buildings after that, although there was an incident where one of

Chester Wilt's haystacks, located on the corner of the Newry ball field, caught on fire. While you may not think a haystack fire was a big deal, this stack was several stories high and created quite a blaze. The cause of this fire was never determined, but it was said that several Newry boys were smoking near the stack and their "activity" got out of hand.

Ches' butcher shop was one of our favorite hangouts in our teen years and we would visit after school, sometimes helping out with odd jobs. I remember one winter evening, just before a holiday, I watched Ches hang a bunch of chickens upside down on a line, slit their throats and let them there until they bled out. Not a pretty site and another of the jobs I crossed off my list as a career!

Christopher Hite, Bill Hite's grandpap, owned a beautiful barn on Pap Hite's farm and one night it caught on fire. Newry, not having a bonafide fire company, had to rely on East Freedom and Duncansville fire companies at the time. As the story goes, late that night word of the fire got to the wife of one of the fire chiefs. She ran to wake the chief and told him, "Get up! Get up! Chris Hite's barn is on fire!" Reportedly he replied, "That's o.k., he can afford it." then rolled over and went back to sleep.

A traumatic accident happened around 1944 that resulted in the loss of a childhood friend and classmate, Eddie Moyer. Eddie lived in Puzzletown and came from a large family, mostly boys who loved the outdoors and hunting. He was about twelve years old and had taken his gun out to hunt rabbits. When he returned home, he hung the still-loaded gun on a rack, where the trigger mechanism caught on a nail and fired. Unfortunately, the shot hit Eddie in the stomach and killed him. Aside from being a good friend, Eddie was also a cousin from the Eger side of the family and was greatly missed by all.

Eddie Moyer

In the early 1940's, brother Jake was enrolled at Hollidaysburg Junior High. While I don't recall many medals or honors being awarded to him for "outstanding accomplishment", he was a member, for a while, of the Model Airplane Club. The boys in this club built lightweight airplanes using balsa wood, rubber bands and airplane glue. Winding the rubber band tight around the propeller would cause the plane to take off (in theory).

Jake said the designers of these airplanes were allowed to hang them in one of the classrooms for display…for a time, a great idea. Then a couple of boys, "accidentally" of course, lit a flame too close to one of the planes and in a flash it and several others hanging from the ceiling became ash! He never told me what the punishment for this accident was, but I don't remember ever hearing of the Model Airplane Club after that!

I kind of idolized Jake as he was rather good looking and liked the girls, who liked him back — a trait he carried with him through numerous relationships and several wives! Not to take liberties with my now deceased brother's character, but if he were alive today I'm sure he could add some "spice" to these writings.

Jake must have thought he knew more than the teachers did, because he didn't last long in high school and the time came when he'd had enough. He and my dad also had their differences, as Dad was a stickler for good work ethics — either you worked or you didn't live under his roof — simple, sound philosophy that should still be used today!

Jake started working for Pap Hite, as did most of my brothers and sisters at one time or another. Looking back, I believe Jake's good attendance record on the farm was due, in part, to a beautiful "incentive"—Marcella Hite, one of Pap's daughters about Jake's

Ralph Hite, all ready to plan corn, 1922

age. I'm sure we can all appreciate job incentives like that!

Pap Hite once allowed Jake to take the old "Oliver" tractor up to Pete Hite's garage for servicing. As the story goes, Jake was standing up to guide the tractor into the front station and apparently hit the gas pedal instead of the brake and went right through the front end of Pete's garage! Thankfully, Jake wasn't hurt and a few days later a sign was posted above the tractor's point of

Pete Hite's garage, 1940.
Later Speed and Bertie Burk's restaurant.

entry that read, "Bomb Damage"!

Another job Jake had was accompanying a Duncansville man who drove a tractor-trailer to the southern states. They would haul potatoes down and then bring fruit back up north. The owner of the rig was Gabriel Rhodes, also known as "Chingapoo". From whence that name was derived, I'm not going to speculate and always hesitated to ask.

They would bring back watermelon, cantaloupe and oranges by the trailer load, and Jake often brought some fruit home with him. With all the hungry, growing boys in our household, these items were always welcome. Fruit was a rare commodity back then, other than the local kind we would "sample" from the neighbors vineyards.

Mr. Rhodes' trips supplied a little market he owned in Cross Keys on the old Sixth Avenue Road. I always envied Jake being able to travel down south, seeing seven or eight states each trip.

Jake also worked at what was known back then as the "County Home for the Poor and Indigent", located on the road between what is now Meadow's Intersection and Plank Road. This building today holds the Hollidaysburg Veterans Home. Jake held a variety of jobs, ranging from being a "runner" for the superintendent, Mr. Craig Berringer, to an attendant who helped care for the elderly housed there.

Sometimes he would take me with him to his job, and I remember being quite shaken at the rows and rows of beds full of men and women and the sad living conditions. I prayed that I would never have to live like that.

Mr. Berringer must have liked Jake because he would frequently send him home with foodstuffs and once, two large boxes of clothing—a mix of shirts, knickers and blouses.

That's where I got my final pair of knickers, likely one of the last boys in Newry to wear them, other than Clete Peck. If there ever was a pair of pants that I hated, it was those County Home knickers.

God bless Mr. Berringer though, as due to his generosity we kids had additional food and warm clothing.

It is in recalling these early days that I am especially thankful for our dear mother, who worked hard to keep us from knowing that we were probably some of the poorest kids in town.

Brother Ray was the next to "test the ire" of my dad as he, too, decided that he was smarter than his high school teachers and quit to gain employment at Pap

Hite's. Again, another pretty Hite girl, Rita, helped make Ray a very dependable employee. Later on, Ray also went to work at the County Home and subsequently retired from the Valley View Home on the boulevard in Altoona.

Hite's Farm

As I mentioned before, all of the Thompson boys at one time or another worked on the Hite farm in a variety of jobs ranging from planting and hoeing crops, shucking corn, bedding cows and horses, and cleaning stables.

One of the dirtiest jobs in the heat of the summer was

Pap Hite's Barn

working in the "hay mow". A wagon full of hay was pulled into the barn and lifted up to the hay mow by means of a large hook and rope-pulley device. One end of the rope would be tied to a horse who would be guided away from the barn until the hook grabbed into a load of hay. It was then lifted to the upper level of the barn where a worker would "trip" the load. Another worker would be up in the mow as the hay was dropped and would spread it around the loft. On occasion the hook would grab too deep into the load, and wagon and all would start rising toward the roof…almost giving Pap Hite a heart attack!

Not the greatest working conditions and as I recall, the pay for this job was about a dollar a day!

Another job that "made a man out of a boy" was filling the silo with silage. This was done using the primitive method of "blowing" the cut silage through a large steel tube that was fastened in sections extending along the outside of the silo.

These were dirty, sweaty jobs and more than convinced me that I wasn't destined to be a farmer!

Along with working the various crops, we were also part of the harvesting crew, which required us to pick tomatoes, lettuce, onions and anything else that grew in the fields. After picking and bunching or crating the crops, they were washed. Looking at Poplar Run today, I'm amazed that more people didn't perish as a result of eating the fruits and vegetables we rinsed in those waters!

My sister Phyllis also contributed her share during those years by picking strawberries on the Hite farm. I believe she started out at a half-cent a quart and on a good day, could probably pick fifty quarts. Eventually strawberry prices rose and the rate for "pickers" went up to a penny a quart!

I also picked my share of strawberries as evidenced by the following photo.

Young Hezzie on fender of
1939 or '40 Chevy on a
Strawberry Picking Day at Hite's Farm

Although Pap Hite kept us all gainfully employed, I also "huckstered" for Earl Hite in the late 1930's and early 40's. He was Pap's brother, and as history has it, they were always feuding. I'm not sure if this was due to family issues or simply a difference in opinion about farming methods.

For reasons long forgotten, I went to work for Earl, loading lettuce, tomatoes, carrots, red beets and any other crop grown on the farm and trucking them to Altoona.

I was really in the "big money" in those days—after three twelve or fourteen hour workdays, I would receive three dollars in cash, no FICA or income tax taken out back then. With that amount of money you could purchase a new pair of shoes at Lasser's, a pair of "overalls", as jeans were called, and probably a shirt, socks and some underwear! If you were really "flush" you could buy a pair of high-top boots that had a leather pocket for carrying a knife. For some reason, owning a pair of these boots raised your status several notches among your friends!

While profitable, an unfortunate consequence of my employment with Earl Hite was that I lost the friendship of the other Hite family, including Joe, Bill, Ferdy and the girls for a time. We eventually resolved our differences and have remained lifelong friends.

Another employer of the Thompson boys was Sam Thomas, the "banana man". Several times a month, tractor-trailer loads of bananas would come into Thomas' fruit market and Paul, Joe and I would get the call to help unload the huge trucks. It was hard work, as those stems of half-green bananas weighed anywhere between twenty-five and seventy-five pounds. We would haul them from the truck and hang them from the ceiling in Sam's store, all the while watching out for the huge tarantula spiders that sometimes clung to the banana stalks. When we'd find one, Sam would carefully put it in a quart jar while reminding us that a tarantula bite usually meant instant death. Believe me, we heeded his warnings. Hauling bananas…another of our "slave labor" jobs for which we received a small hourly wage and probably a stalk of bananas!

SCHOOL DAYS

During the early years, St. Patrick's School was a two-story frame and stucco building, with a convent on the second floor that housed up to six

Old St. Pat's School, est 1921

Sisters of Mercy. Facing the building, first and second grades were located in the left wing and third through sixth grades were in the center section, which also held a large stage where many "professional" musicals and plays were performed. The right wing was the seventh and eighth grade classroom.

There was also a cement block outhouse with two sides, one for the boys and one for the girls. The girls side held two old ceramic toilets (no flushers!) with wooden seats and the same on the boys side. The boys side had the lovely addition of a urinal the size of a watering trough.

The Sisters of Mercy had "real" bathrooms in their convent, but I don't remember ever having the use of their facilities!

St. Pat's was blessed to have the fine teaching skills of a number of nuns back then, including Sisters Mary Jean, Mary Agnes, Mary Protase, Mary Alban, Mary Patrice, Mary Victoria, Mary Bonaventure, Mary Avila and Sister Mary Louise, the Principal.

I remember wondering why they were all named Mary, and just figured it was because there were so many of them they ran out of names!

Sister Mary John Stevens was a music teacher and organist early in the history of St. Pat's School. She was said to be very devoted, young and beautiful. Tragically, she died in 1923 in the choir loft during Mass. Her parents, Mr. and Mrs. N. A. Stevens, donated a statue of Bernadette Soubirous to the St. Pat's grotto in honor of their daughter.

Sister Mary Jean McCann taught first and second grade and her room overlooked the playground and Poplar Run. Her dad, Judge McCann, served on the Court in Cambria County, and was known for meting out severe punishments during his tenure. I soon discovered that his daughter, the nun, inherited her father's traits for administering justice! I'm sure Sister didn't consider me one of her prize students, and I in turn, was not very fond of her teaching methods.

I was born a "lefty" and wrote left-handed. Well, the Sister in all her wisdom, thought that young Francis should write right-handed, so with the help of a "teaching aid", a three-foot ruler, she taught me to write with my right hand. I never could understand why those nuns were called "Sisters of Mercy" when they all ruled with a big stick!

Judging by my penmanship today, she should have left well enough alone! Of course, I can also attribute this to a seventy-plus year old arthritic hand, much like my mother, who suffered severely with "stiff" hands, as she called them.

Sister Mary Jean and I had a few good "go rounds" as I recall. One day she caught me chewing gum in music class and suggested that I stand in the corner in front of the class with the offending gum stuck to the end of my nose. Having inherited the prominent "Thompson" proboscis, it was obvious to the class what sin I had committed. Unfortunately, Sister heard me chuckle when given my punishment and decided that Francis wasn't remorseful enough, so she ordered me to go to the rectory to see the good Pastor, Jeremiah P. Flynn. I pleaded my case to him ... and lost, if memory serves me. Thankfully, in this instance I was spared an introduction to his method of enforcement, a barbaric wooden paddle that leaned against the wall in his office.

All of the kids felt that the "discipline" doled out by the nuns and Father Flynn bordered on child abuse, but looking back, I'm sure it was just their way of taking the proper corrective measures in an attempt to bring us "closer to God"!

Although I could be mistaken, I can only recall being on the receiving end of that infamous paddle once in my school tenure, after Don "Monk" Conrad coerced me into playing hooky with him. We snuck off the school grounds and headed over to Addie Hoover's store. I believe I had made it the whole way over the hedge and

Monk about halfway, when a big black Buick pulled up and out sprung our sainted Pastor. Of course, he

immediately inquired as to why we were out climbing hedges instead of in our classroom learning. After sputtering some dumb excuse, we were ushered into the back seat of the big Buick and taken to the rectory for our punishment. On the tense ride back, Monk whispered to me to scream and cry as soon as the first whack was administered, thinking this would lessen the number. I

The Reverend Jeremiah P. Flynn
1945

did…and it didn't. Father Flynn, it seems, was familiar with this ploy and therefore immune to the pleas of a young truant.

My desire to play hooky was greatly diminished after this incident and it wouldn't be until high school that I would attempt it again!

I don't know where "Monk" got his nickname, but I'm sure it held no connotation to a monastic life, as he was always an ornery kid. He was cared for by his four or five brothers after his mother and father passed away early in his life. Monk, although older than me, was a good buddy and a true friend.

On one occasion, though, he made not have been on my side. He, Don Burk, Jim Stalter and I were playing down at the "cesspool", this being the above ground septic system for St. Pat's School. Hardly legal or environmentally safe, even in those days, it was utilized at the time for obvious purposes. Anyway, we boys got into a rock battle, throwing at each other from across the cesspool, and Monk conked me one on the back of the head as I was retreating. I still have the scar and never fail to show it to him when I see him…naturally he denies the whole incident.

I guess I wasn't the only one with friends like this. There's a story about when Biggie Bo Bogel, Woody Thompson & Prig Burkey shaved Paul and George Burk's heads, then fed them ExLax, telling them that it was chocolate candy!

The playground at St. Pat's with its seesaws and swings provided us rowdy boys with an outlet for our excess energy. The swings were anchored by huge posts, most likely utility poles about thirty feet high. One of life's earliest goals was to swing so high that you went over the top, and several of the more daring guys were masters of this feat.

One memorable event on the playground occurred the day I snuck several of my brother Ray's metal darts with me to school. Knowing they were "contraband", I hid them until recess. Using a swing pole as a target, I was demonstrating my dart-throwing prowess when one dart missed the mark and landed at Mary Catherine Burket's feet. She, in turn, picked it up and threw it back, where it hit me squarely in the chest. The dart stuck, and hurt like heck, but the wound wasn't serious. Sister Mary Jean was nearby and gently removed the

"All Star Team" 1946. First row-Don Glass, Robert Noel, Tom Sutch, Joe Culp, Floyd Lanzendorfer, Ed Eger. Second row-Pat Bradley, Lester Weise, Ray Dodson, Ray Marcinko. Rear left-Unkown, Don Burk. Middle-Hezzie Thompson.

Must have been a sale on plaid coats in 1946!
Front row-Morrison, Joe Thompson, Schmidhammer. Second row-Morrison, Jim Thompson, Sell, unknown, unknown, Dewey Thompson, Ott, unknown, Don Bradley, Reilly. Third row-Don Bem, John Wilt, Mike Kelly, unknown, Joe Dodson, Bob Sell, Popeye Thompson, Larry Stalter, Chuck Wilt. Fourth row-Ed Eger, Ray Marcinko, Ray Dodson, Floyd Lanzendorfer, Bob Noel, Joe Culp, Les Weise.

First row-Jim Thompson.
Second row-Ed Eger, Floyd Lanzendorfer, Ray Marcinko.
Third row-Ray Dodson.
Top-Donny Bradley, 1946.

dart…with one quick yank.

Needless to say, I caught hell from all corners, first from the good Sister and then from Ray, who probably never saw his darts again.

I imagine Sister Mary Jean, along with the other sainted Sisters from St. Pat's, spent a good deal of their "time with the Lord" praying for our safety and welfare, but I can't say as we returned the favor. We seemed to delight in making their lives as eventful as possible, and therein lies my next story.

Sparrows liked to roost in the eaves of a small cellarway in Addie and Tommy Hoover's store, making it very easy to catch them. One evening, a couple of evil-

St. Pat's School, 1942. Grades Three and Four. First row-Ed Moyer, Paul Muri, Ray Dodson, Rosemary Burket, Hezzie Thompson, Pat Bradley, Louise Kelly, Ellen Reilly, Eleanor Reilly. Second row-Tom Sutch, Helen Dodson, Don Burk, Frank Horvath, Joe Hite, Peanuts Billotte, Mary Elizabeth Glass, Barbara McAlee. Third row-Jim Stalter, Bob Eger, Bob Moses, Floyd Lanzendorfer, Laura Jane Ritchey, Margaret Zeth, Rita Zeth, Mary Catherine Wyant, Marjorie Hite. Fourth row-Monk Conrad, Jane Frances Hite, Betty Kelly, Mary Gloria Boyer, Mary Catherine Burket, Ginny Wilt. Top row-Fr. Flynn, Jeanne George.

minded boys caught a sparrow and took it down to St. Pat's church, where they placed it in the old organ up in the choir loft.

Knowing that Sister Mary Jean was deathly afraid of birds, this group of scofflaws could hardly wait until the next morning when, at eight a.m. Mass, Sister would lift the lid of the organ and that poor frightened sparrow would fly out. She did, and it took off, scaring her half to death. From then on, Sister always made sure she was first to the choir loft for Mass, and always peeked in the organ before opening it!

I don't know if the culprits ever confessed to this crime, but I do know that I was very sorry.

St. Pat's School. Grades First and Second. First row-Ruth Glass, Anne Sell, Edna Zeth, Carol Sipes, Mary Jane Bradley, Dodson, Colleen Dodson, Denise Gonsman, Reilly, Donna Moses, Dory Kelly. Second row-Barbara Fox, Rita Lanzendorfer, Lois Hite, Elizabeth McAlee, Charlie Reilly, Carl Moses, Bill Hite, Popeye Thompson, Bill Culp, Bob Moyer, Paul Burk, Bud Burket. Third row-Dolores Gonsman, Louise Moyer, Robert Zeth, Ed Eger, Joe Culp, Jim Burk, Don Moyer, John Sell, Chuck Wilt, Don Glass, Carl Wyant. Top: Sr. Mary Jean

One of the boys who pulled the sparrow prank was my friend, Paul "Dinky" Muri. Dinky was very protected as a child, as his sisters Marcella and Marie

and brother Lou kept pretty good tabs on him. Early on, he and I became "blood brothers", using the Indian method of cutting our wrists to join blood and vowing never to tell anyone about our secret pact. We remained the best of friends through high school, hanging out and double-dating. We both married and had kids, and renewed our friendship when I sold him a home in

Paul (Dinky) Muri

Altoona in the 1960's. I was Uncle Hezzie to his kids and he was Uncle Paul to mine. To this day, the second generation of Muri kids still give Uncle Hezzie and Aunt Charleen a big hug when they see us.

Paul's early death from brain cancer in 1974 left a terrible void in all our lives, and I still miss him. Relationships like ours were few and far between.

I started school at St. Pat's a year or so after we moved to the big white house between Newry and Catfish, and along with my siblings had to walk about a mile to school, as the old saying goes, "uphill both ways". We would leave home early every morning to get to Mass, and I recall trying to find heavy clothes and socks without holes an everyday chore.

Being one of twelve kids, I learned early, as did my

brothers and sisters, that there were some concessions to be made, socks being one of them. My dear mother probably washed a hundred pairs of socks a week for nine very rough and tumble boys, and even with all of her sewing and sorting, socks without holes were a premium. I'm not sure which of my brothers wore out the toes and which wore out the heels, but as a result, by the end of the week I usually had to wear two pair to cover both heels and toes!

I also wore "knickers" back then and recall on more than one occasion having to use Ball jar rings to hold those knickers up to my knees. I once tore a hole in a pair of brown knickers and knew that my Mother

When Knickers Brought No Snickers

Remember when these lengthy shorts were patched and pants were "pegged"?

wouldn't let me wear them with a hole, and was just as sure that she probably wouldn't have a patch to match. Sure enough, she patched those brown knickers with a blue patch...lesson learned, be more careful with your clothes. Oh, how I hated those wearing those pants!

Mom didn't like her boys to wear uncreased

"overalls", so she always made sure to iron one in before we were allowed to wear them. Also, we boys disliked wearing pants with a wide leg, so she spent many an hour trimming and "pegging" our pants. Another fond memory I hold of my mother and how hard she worked to keep us happy.

I was such a little guy when I went to first grade, barely past my fifth year. I wasn't very fond of this business of sitting in a seat for the whole day, and remember once heading for home at recess. My mother, in her convincing fashion, sent me right back to school—and that was the end of that!

Two horrible memories from this time still come to mind — that of contracting whooping cough and the awful medicine I had to take. I can recall having a terrible coughing spell while I was sitting at our living room window and as a result, slipped and broke the window…it's strange what memories "stick", isn't it?

Another illness I had as a child was a nervous condition where I couldn't sit still, then known as St. Vitus Dance. (I guess now they call it Attention Deficit Disorder) The condition was so bad that I couldn't go to school for a while and missed part of first grade, having to repeat that whole year. Sister Mary Jean was probably glad to see me go because I'm sure I disrupted the whole class!

Years later, I asked my mother how I recovered from this disease and she told me that our doctor mixed a "tonic" for me, the chief ingredient being "Tincture of Bella Donna". If this condition had any lasting effects, in my case it left me with a weakness in both eyes. As a result, I blinked constantly, a problem I have to this day. It's been embarrassing at times and has always made me very self-conscious.

There weren't many family doctors back in those days, but two of the names that stay with me are Dr. Grounds in Roaring Spring and Dr. Charles Johnson in Claysburg.

My mother also told me about an accident that I had when I was three or four years old. I tumbled down some stairs and ended up falling against a red-hot coal stove—one of the old potbellied ones. Several layers of skin on both hands were severely damaged and again, one of those great country practitioners mixed a salve that my mother had to place between the layers of infected tissue. She wasn't satisfied with the good doctor's diagnosis that I would never again have use of my hands and made me exercise with a little ball until I regained the use of both of them. As I write these words I once again thank God for a gentle, loving mother who took time to make me well while still caring for the other seven children at home at the time.

Looking back I need not wonder why I am such a nervous guy—I had a couple of pretty good "shots" back then.

One of the most tragic incidents during my school career occurred in March of 1944 when St. Pat's School and Convent burned to the ground. This old building was a two-story wood frame with stucco on the outside.

As I've said before in these writings, the Convent was located on the second floor and was the primary residence for the Sisters of Mercy. I doubt if many people ever had the privilege of entering the nuns' domain, and I'm sure when darkness fell, those convent doors were bolted. I don't believe I ever saw any of the Sisters out at night. This is a far cry from today's "brand" of religious, who have become such an integral part of the communities in which they live.

The devastating fire affected many lives, mine among them. We kids couldn't believe our eyes as we ran up the road from our house to witness the flames and smoke pouring from the school. The old building had oiled wood floors and an ancient roof that I'm sure went up like tinder. The effect could be seen for miles.

The local fire companies had little opportunity to salvage anything, but fortunately the nuns were all able to get out safely. Looking back now on this sad event, I realize that the good Sisters in all probability lost all of their worldly possessions in their haste to escape the fire, this of a time and age when a "vow of poverty" meant just that.

I can still remember walking around the smoky, stench-filled ruins with several other kids trying to save anything of value. We were able to find a few coins from the remains of one of the Sister's desks, most likely from the "Pagan Baby Fund", a long-standing Catholic tradition…I've often wondered if any of those pagan babies ever embraced the Faith.

A special find of mine was an old skeleton key, soot covered and charred by the flames. Seeing Sister Mary

Alban surveying the loss, I went over and proudly presented her with it, which she accepted gratefully. I guess she and I sort of bonded over the years. Later in life, when she resided at St. Mary's Convent on Sixth Avenue in Altoona, Don Burk and I made several trips to see her. We corresponded for several years into the 1950's and her familiar closing statement in each letter was as follows, "You be a good boy, Francis!" I'm sure she prayed for me, and the good Lord must have been listening, as here I am these many years later.

In addition to Sister Mary Jean, Sister Mary Alban and I also shared a few "memorable" moments when she taught me in fourth or fifth grade. Once when Sister was out of the room briefly, the perfect opportunity arose to launch a paper airplane. Someone did (I'd imagine Dinky Muri or Pat Bradley, as they really knew how to make those airplanes sail!) and it landed right on Sister Mary Alban's desk.

Pious lad that I was, I was attempting to retrieve the plane so that no one got in trouble, when Sister reappeared. Thinking that the perpetrator of this crime was young Francis Thompson, Sister leaned down (all 250 pounds of her) and hoisted me into the air! As she did, several buttons on my shirt popped off and there I stood, looking like "Fat Stuff" from the Joe Palooka comic strip...one button on and four on the floor.

Petrified, I tried to plead my innocence, but soon realized that I had already been tried and convicted by way of the "NCS", the Nuns Court System. Knowing that my sentence was imminent, I tried one last ploy and blurted out something to the effect that my mother was not going to be pleased when I returned home with only one button on my shirt. Wrong move.

Sister Mary Alban, in no uncertain terms, straightened me out… "You, young man, will stay after school and sew those buttons back on your shirt!" I did exactly that, and to this day I'm still pretty good at sewing on buttons.

As a result of this encounter with Sister, I gained much respect for her and her considerable "strength". Sister's glasses always slid down her nose when she was challenged and needless to say, I tried from that day on not to be the cause of those glasses' descent!

After St. Pat's burned down, my brothers and I had to go to the "Pike School", located between Newry and Sam Thomas' market. Again, this was prior to school buses, so our transportation was foot power and where we lived made this daily trek quite a task. As there was no real road from our house to the school, we had to go through the woods past "Boogie" Benton's peach orchard, then up toward John Weyant's and down Gray's Lane just to get to school in the morning. Although it would've been easier for us to go to public school in Newry, the fact was we lived in Blair Township and school enrollments were governed by boundary guidelines.

Pike School was a small two-story brick edifice, having a coal and wood furnace and no running water. There was a frame outhouse out back complete with the luxury of a "two-holer", one for the boys and one for the girls. Due to the lack of inside plumbing, the students took turns walking along old Route 220 to the "Halfway House", where we would fill the buckets from a water pump and lug them back to school. The location of this property was halfway between Newry and Duncansville, thus the name.

Our teacher was a maiden lady by the name of Sarah Lightner. Looking back now, I believe she may have acquired her teaching certificate by virtue of a correspondence course, as our "curriculum" consisted of reviewing Life Magazine and a few other periodicals of the era!

Some of the students I attended school with were Cloyd and Denny Smith and their sisters, the Thomas kids, and Jean and Dick Gray among others. Whitey and Mary Catherine Weyant traversed the rural route with us every day, too.

Of course, my time at the Pike School was not without incident, one of which occurred during recess. A classmate of mine, Lillian Johnston (whose name I'll never forget) took occasion to use the outhouse and "someone" slipped a piece of wood through the outside door handle, thereby locking Lillian inside. The recess bell rang, and all of the students went back to class. In time, the teacher discovered Lillian's absence and sent someone to find her. They did...still locked in the outhouse.

I forgot to mention that Lillian, while only in fourth or fifth grade, was 5'2" and probably 150 pounds. Well, when Lillian was released and somehow informed that

Francis Thompson was the culprit, I was in big trouble! At her earliest convenience, Lillian attacked me and pummeled me to the ground. It took me quite a while to recover as I recall.

I've always wondered where Lillian ended up in life. Maybe she became a professional wrestler!

Our tenure at Pike School was short, and Life Magazine 101 came to an end when our family moved back in town to Newry.

As the new St. Pat's School was not yet completed, the Newry Public School was the next to be "blessed" with the Thompson boys' presence. This was a modern two-room school with coal and wood pipeless furnaces or heater stoves. (Can you tell from my descriptions that I spent a lifetime selling real estate?)

These years were pretty tough for the kids from St. Pat's, being that we were subject to all the different schools and rules, but we survived. I doubt we

Newry Public School

"Catholic kids" even made it into the class pictures as we weren't there long enough to be included, and I'm sure the teachers weren't sorry to see us go!

The best part of this experience was gaining the friendship of Gene Paul "Pete" Cassidy and Boyd "Spit" Shaw, along with many of the guys who have remained my friends over the past seventy years or so.

In January of 1945, almost a year after the fire, most of the Catholic kids returned to the new St. Pat's school, which, for some reason, had been constructed smack in the middle of our ball field. Believe me, we weren't too happy about that!

The new school was one of the finest one-story brick buildings in the area with an abundance of natural lighting by virtue of numerous large windows…and of course I have a story tied to those windows. As it happened, one day I was caught misbehaving, (it's slipped my memory as to the actual deed), and was given the punishment by one of the nuns to wash all of

the classroom windows in the entire school! Fortunately, two other miscreants were being punished at the same time, so we shared the labor.

New St.Pat's School reopened in January 1945

A beautiful outdoor grotto had been built beside the church and was the scene of the annual May crowning of the blessed Mary. The young girls of St. Pat's Sodality vied for the coveted title of May Queen every year. The Queen was "crowned" on the roof of the grotto and the affair was always a wonderful day for our little church.

The Grotto at St.Pat's Church

An early May crowning in front of the Grotto

Another annual event was the St. Pat's picnic, with the men from the church laboring long hours to erect the large canvas tents and numerous wooden church tables for the booths.

Father Flynn was a gracious boss and one of the perks for the workers was the cold keg waiting in the church basement (necessitating quite a few trips there by the men throughout the day!) Occasionally after picnic hours, the men would gather at the rectory to indulge in a bit of the "hard stuff"—the ladies of the parish oft times having to rescue their husbands and return them home.

We kids always looked forward to the picnic, most likely only having a dime to spend, but able to make it last all day. Dad, and Paul and I had our picture taken

by a fellow with a big box camera on a stand and a hand-held flash.

Recalling the picnic always brings to mind my dad and Pius Kelly and many others working the games of chance. A popular game consisted of a big

Dad with Popeye and Hezzie
St. Pat's Picnic, 1937

wooden board laid out flat, with "pigeon holes" on the surface, each with a corresponding number. Players would place their money and bet on their favorite space, then the operator would yell out, "Round and round he goes, no one knows where Mickey Mouse goes!" and would release a live mouse that would scurry across the board. Scared half to death, the mouse would bolt down one of the numbered holes and the "owner" of that hole won all the money that had been bet, except for the small house payment for the parish.

The picnic was held every August during harvesting time for wheat and corn crops, the connection being that the mice for the "Mickey Mouse" game were culled from the nests they built under the sheaves of both. The local boys would go down to Pap Hite's farm to gather the mice for the game. A dime a mouse, and if I remember correctly, I earned more than a few dimes for my catches.

I'm sure the church made plenty of money on this and other ingenious games, but this one in particular always intrigued me. An observation—in this day and age, animal rights advocates like PETA would have the game operator in court for the "mistreatment" of animals, and I'm sure the Walt Disney Empire would sue for name infringement...life was so simple back then!

The annual St. Patrick's Festival continues to this day and is attended by many residents, both former and current, and a good time is had by all.

I'll close my chapter on our early school days with a memory provided by my sister Phyllis. It seems that she, Lois Weaver and Aileen Flynn (Father Flynn's niece) needed one more prank to fill their "Halloween bag" one year, so they decided to soap all of the convent windows. All three snuck down to the convent and went to work. Things were going great and they could hardly contain themselves as they moved from one window to another, soap in hand, when they looked up and there stood a good Sister looking out at them!

The three "stooges" learned their fate the next day in school. The punishment, of course, was washing every window in the convent...all fifty or sixty of them.

Saint Pat's

The town of Newry

WAR STORIES

Our Dedicated Servicemen

On December 7, 1941, the Japanese attacked Pearl Harbor and the war that resulted impacted our little community along with many others across the country.

As town historians have frequently noted, our local borough supplied the Armed Services with more than its share of men and women. The Newry Bicentennial Commemorative booklet states that quite a few Newry men also served in the Civil War and World War I.

Many an anxious mother prayed for her child's safety during these years and there are numerous photos of these brave men and women standing tall in their uniforms. Service men and women held a special place in the hearts of the Newry residents and the annual Decoration Day service held at our Catholic cemetery was attended by those of varied faiths to honor our deceased veterans.

We also had an outdoor Mass on the cemetery grounds and the honor guard would fire their M1 Garand rifles over the graves. As a small boy, I would scramble to retrieve the spent shell casings, not realizing that some ten or twelve years later my friends and I would be firing one of those heavy rifles during basic training in the Korean War.

James E. VanZandt would speak at a memorial service held at the Newry Public School. At the time, he was one of the country's most famous Navy personnel, I believe a Lieutenant Commander, and would later become a distinguished U. S. Congressman. I had the honor of meeting him when he hosted a four-day visit to Washington, D.C. for high school students that I attended as the representative of Hollidaysburg High

School for the 1948 International Relations Club.

Although my brothers and I and other "young bucks" weren't yet old enough to serve our country, our contribution was that of war effort collections.

One such project was the collection of milkweed pods, which we kids would gather into large bags and a man by the name of Sid Koch would come around and collect them. I believe we received twenty-five cents for each bag. According to the locals, milkweed pods were used as sort of a synthetic material and processed as fill for use by the military.

Mr. Koch also hired us to pick elderberries, which were used to make jelly for the soldiers. A big truck would come down the road and pick up the bags, and again I think the pay was twenty-five cents a bag.

Scrap collection was another war effort project and if memory serves, also a Boy Scout activity. Kids would gather scrap iron and take it to the old warehouse behind Pauly Beigle's store. We had a mountain of scrap ranging from old bicycles to stoves, car parts, metal iceboxes and some other items that even we weren't sure what they were.

The scrap metal warehouse was the scene of one of my earliest "battle scars". One day a couple of us guys were separating the scrap and someone, I think it was Don Burk, picked up a part from an old cast iron pitcher pump and asked where it should go, as cast iron was kept separate from regular iron. He was told to throw it in a certain pile, which he did. Unfortunately, I happened to be in the line of flight, and it conked me on the head. Blood flew and I blacked out. When I came to, the guys were taking me to Sadie Hite's for treatment. A little peroxide and a bandage was administered, and it was back to the junk pile...such compassion!

The Conrad family had four sons who served. They lost their son, Adam, who I believe was the only serviceman from Newry to die in this terrible war. The Lanzendorfer family from Puzzletown had five sons in the military and lost one, Earl. Glenn Conrad and his three brothers served in the military and fortunately, all returned home safely.

Adam Conrad   *Earl J. Lanzendorfer*

BUY WAR BONDS

Jake

Hezzie

Paul

My mother was proud of the fact that six of her sons, Jake, Paul, Joe, Butch, Babe and I served in the military over the years. Mom always found time to write to each of us despite her arthritic hands. God bless you Mom!

Joe

Butch

Babe

Joe, Paul, Hezzie, 1953

Paul

Babe

Butch and a buddy

Hezzie and Casper Schmidt
Ft. Campbell, Kentucky
1953

Rita

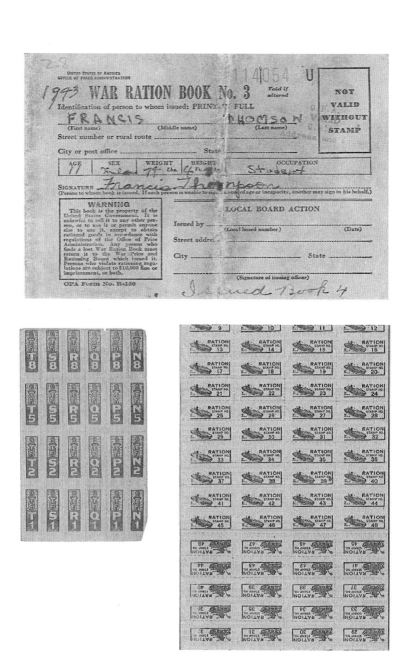

My ration book and stamps 1943

The war years were not easy ones for any family, especially large ones, due to the necessity of food and meat rationing. While compiling this journal, I came across my original ration book, along with several red and blue tokens that were used as change if you didn't use the full value of the ration stamp.

Among the various items rationed was oleo margarine, which was sealed in a one-pound bag. It was bland in color and came with a small colored "button" that was blended in with the margarine, rendering it yellow. I'd imagine anyone who could afford "real" butter back then wouldn't have known of this magic little button!

A type of bartering system became necessary for our family, large as it was. Shoes were included in the rationing process, as leather was used for the war effort. My dad decided we didn't have use for all of the shoe stamps in each kid's book, so he would swap shoe stamps with the neighbors for meat stamps. Although bartering was against the rules of the Office of Price Administration or OPA, and the rationing board, it was common practice for families with lots of mouths to feed.

In our house, you had one pair of shoes for everyday use, including Sunday. If you worked, you might have two pairs, as Dad did, and those shoes had to last until the next ration stamp became eligible (if it wasn't already traded for meat, that is!)

As I've stated before, our small town produced many dedicated servicemen, evidenced by photos of the guys on leave from their various branches. They would come home dressed in their best parade uniforms and wore their stripes and medals proudly. I can only recall two girls who served in the military, Agnes Gonsman and Anna Mae Benton, who were nurses and thankfully, returned home unharmed.

World War II was really going strong in 1944, and my dad and many other railroad workers stepped up and labored long hours in support of the war effort. My dad was very dedicated to "The Company" (the Pennsylvania Railroad) and my mom told us boys stories of how he had experienced serious injuries, among them a partially crushed foot and a crippling injury to one of his hands. Early on in his career he also suffered the loss of an eye and used a glass eye until he died.

The irony of these horrible injuries was that my dad, being so loyal to the PRR, always settled the injury claims for a token amount of money.

I guess he expected the same of his boys as well. In 1959, I was working the second shift at the old Hollidaysburg Reclamation Plant and severely lacerated my finger working on railroad material. After weeks of excellent medical care, I met with the "claims agent", a guy no one ever wanted to deal with, along with the union rep who negotiated the claim. My dad heard of the meeting and point blank told me that I had better settle for what they offered me! I knew anything other than this option meant that I would incur the wrath of my father…end result, I settled.

The years during the war only contributed to the

small town atmosphere and brought its residents closer, as the daily talk at the old Wonder Bar, Piney McCoy's and Addie and Tommy Hoover's store was of where the local sons and daughters were stationed, how they were faring, and more importantly, when they were coming home. Due to our living on Catfish Road for a time, I didn't get to see many of the servicemen, but heard lots of war stories, a few of which are still passed around to this day.

Several years ago, Glenn and Wayne Conrad and several older Newry guys started a "Newry Guys Breakfast" which has grown into a bi-monthly breakfast club held at various local restaurants. We average twelve to fourteen guys a meeting and it's become a great opportunity to renew old friendships and reminisce a bit. Most of us are in our seventies and eighties, but the stories about "girls" still abound! I'm sure some of the "younger guys", the fifty and sixty-year olds, doubt the veracity of most of these escapades, but don't hesitate to add their own. Some of the milder versions I have included in this journal, along with the shared history of our little town.

Newry Guys Breakfast 2003

Our house on the "main drag" - Bedford Street

Around 1944, our family moved from the house on Catfish back to Newry, right on the main road. The house we moved into was previously occupied by two families, the Moses' and the Pringle's, who were somehow related to us, according to family history. As our family totaled ten or so at the time, we took over the entire dwelling!

The domestic water source for this house was a well that was located out from the rear porch and had a metal pump from which we drew our water. It worked well in the warmer months, but in the winter had to be "primed" by dumping hot water over the top of it. Back then a hot water heater was a luxury, so we had to heat all of our water on the old coal and wood stove in the kitchen. The water pump was later moved into the kitchen, making it somewhat easier for Mom to care for our large family. Occasionally, even this water system would freeze up and on frigid mornings we would have to thaw the pipes to the kitchen.

We were still without an inside bathroom, so bathing was quite a chore. We would heat the bath water on the stove and pour it in a basin, then carry it to our bedroom for a "sponge bath" in as much privacy as ten inhabitants would allow!

Jim, Hezzie, Dewey, Paul

Bedroom space was also somewhat limited, with one of the three bedrooms being occupied by Mom and Dad, one by Phyllis (oh, the perks of womanhood!) and one large bedroom that held my brothers Paul, Joe, Jim, Butch, Dewey, Babe and me. As I recall, choice of bed occupancy came by virtue of age—older boys had their choice of beds (hardly Sealy Posture-pedics), and we rarely slept less than three to a bed.

Heat was supplied by a coal-fired, pipeless furnace located in the dirt-floored basement, which meant our "central heat" was conveyed through a large hole cut into the floor above the furnace and covered with a metal grate or register. Heat to the second floor was accessed by another hole located in the large bedroom occupied by the boys.

Today my brothers and I often kid about our sleeping arrangements, but we grew as a family in closeness...not out of desire, but necessity.

With all the kids in the house, my mother was busy baking homemade bread, a week's supply usually totaling forty loaves or so, plus a cake or two. She told of once having baked several loaves of bread (coating each with oleo and covering them with a cloth used for this purpose) and placing them on the kitchen table after supper. I believe it was Raymond (I'm sure it couldn't have been Paul or I!) who came home with a few friends after Mom went to bed and cut the ends off each loaf to make sandwiches. Needless to say, unless wrapped in waxed paper, the bread would harden by morning, and it did. About the only thing it was good for was dipping in coffee or milk.

I remember feeling bad for the "city" kids at school who never got homemade bread sandwiches...I can also recall selling quite a few of mine for a dime!

My sister Phyllis relates that when our family was in need of milk, she would walk down to Pap Hite's house in Newry and Mrs. Hite (Sadie) would siphon off two glass jugs of milk out of the big metal cans brought up from the farm.

We were glad to be back with our buddies in town, and never lacked for things to do. As I have stated before, entertainment was always an "as you make it" venture, and we used to gather at Addie and Tommy Hoover's store on the lower diamond to hang out. Hoover's store literally had anything one could want. The walls were stacked high with shelves and drawers were packed with merchandise.

A favorite game of ours was "wits". The game began when one kid picked out an item by sight and challenged the other kids to locate and name that item. We could play this game for hours, or at least until Addie or Tommy would "usher" the participants outside.

Hoover's had a lunchmeat and cheese section with their refrigeration consisting of an ice chest under the counter. If we hadn't bought our lunchmeat at Shaw's already, we would go to Hoover's because my dad had a "bill" there. Be it known that on payday this was the first account to be settled!

One day I was delegated to go buy the cheese for Dad's lunch, so I made the trip to Hoover's store. When I gave Mr. Hoover my order for a quarter's worth of cheese, I swear I saw him scoot a big old cat's butt off the

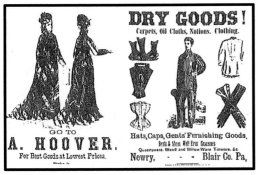

Hoover's Store

cheese block, then cut my dad's order from it...I never told my dad about the incident, but I resolved to eat only peanut butter and jelly sandwiches from then on!

Glenn Conrad told me the story of an elderly fellow by the name of Johnny Mack who worked at Leighty's Market and roomed in Newry. He was reported to take a can of sardines to work each day and always kept the empty can.

Leighty's Fruit Stand, est 1909

Glenn says that when Mr. Mack died, bushel baskets full of sardine cans were found in his room...so I guess you could say Johnny Mack started "recycling" in Newry!

We had more than a few eccentric neighbors when we lived in Newry, one being a nice old gentleman who lived next door to us, "Cap" Hodge, a former Navy man. Wilse Benton told me that Cap built the brick house next to us on Catfish Road, then later moved to Newry. I don't remember a Mrs. Hodge, but the boys tell me Cap had a pretty daughter named Mary.

Mr. Hodge was a janitor for St. Pat's Church and School and also farmed a small piece of land down by the Newry creek. One year Mr. Hodge planted cantaloupes and by harvest time had a bumper crop of nice ripe fruit. From what I've "heard", a group of ornery Newry boys got into that patch and ruined the entire crop. Now, I was pretty close to one of the culprits and can't figure out why we would've thrown some of those fine cantaloupes in the creek and smashed the rest! The end result of this deed was that those four or five boys worked for Cap Hodge the rest of that summer.

Years later, when Mr. Hodge was our neighbor, we became friends and I always prayed that he didn't have a good recollection of the boys from the "cantaloupe incident"!

We also lived next door to an elderly couple named Bob and Alice Nichols. Being childless, I'm sure they didn't relish the thought of eight or nine Thompson kids moving into the neighborhood!

Mrs. Nichols was the proud owner of a Pekinese dog, who I swear was the ugliest dog I had ever seen. This dog was low to the ground, about two feet long, and had two fang-like teeth jutting from its mouth. His name was "Chauncey". Well, I suspect that Chauncey got his share of taunting and teasing from the boys next door, which I'm sure didn't endear us any further to Mrs. Nichols. Looking back at the things we did to that dog, it's a wonder it survived!

Mr. Nichols was a stately white-haired gentleman with a handsome white mustache, and had the role in Newry government of a "Burgess". To this day I don't know what a Burgess did, but I remember Mr. Nichols flaunted his esteemed position throughout the neighborhood.

The Nichols had a beautiful sedan car called a Cortland, which they kept housed in a frame garage down the alley behind our house. Mr. Nichols took great pride in this car and kept it in tip-top shape. As he only drove it on clear, dry days, the immaculate wooden spoke wheels were never touched by mud or grime.

…What, you were waiting for a "story"? Sorry, none to tell, although I find that hard to believe myself!

Another neighbor, "Doody" Benton, was a real character and the grandfather of Wilse and Harry Benton. When I questioned the name "Doody", Wilse told me that in Mr. Benton's youth, he would get all dressed up in his best clothes to go out and the guys would say, "Look at that dude!" Thus the name, and it stuck, like all good Newry nicknames do. Mr. Benton was also called "Colonel", I suppose due to some prior military service.

One day Pete Cassidy and I, all of nine or ten years old, were visiting Doody and he invited us to join him in a chew of tobacco. Chew back then consisted of chunks of ugly brown tobacco cut from a plug, usually Five Brothers, Cuttypipe or Redman. Whatever the brand, Pete and I accepted his offer and put that nasty stuff in our mouths. Following Doody's example, we started to chew. And chew. Being that we didn't see him spit the "juice" in a can, as was the norm for practiced chewers, Pete and I opted to do the same. I don't remember where Pete unloaded his stomach, but I didn't make it too far from the back door…and my tobacco-chewing career was over before it began.

My mom's dad, Grandpap Leonard, chewed

tobacco and when he came to visit I knew I could always earn a few pennies by procuring a spit can for him. He'd tell me to be careful not to throw the juice away, as it was said to be a sure cure for "cow itch" or athlete's foot, but I don't recall ever having saved that magic potion after Grandpap went home!

Mom's Dad
Pap Leonard
1945

Pap and Jake
sampling the
brew
1928

During the war years, most of the cigarettes went to the servicemen, so if you wanted a "smoke", you'd gather up some cornsilk from the top of a cornstalk and wrap it in a piece of the Altoona Mirror. My sister Phyllis and her friend Lois Weaver were probably the best cornsilk cigarette rollers in town. Around this time, The Bugler Tobacco Company invented a "roll your own" cigarette machine, and if you had one of these little hand-held contraptions you could make a lot of money just rolling cigs for your friends. I doubt there are very many of these gadgets still around, and if there are, they are probably worth a fortune on the antique market. Cigarettes back then cost anywhere from eleven to fifteen cents a pack and the handroller brought the cost down to just pennies a pack.

Newry, like any other small town, lacked many places for kids to hang out, but in the late 1930's and early 40's, there was a weekly movie shown in Pauly Beigle's store. Admission was probably five cents or so, and though there were no soda, popcorn or candy concessions to load up on before the show, no one cared as long as we got to see Tom Mix, Johnny Mack Brown, Red Ryder and the Lone Ranger every week. Life was great!

Beigle's store had a large grate in the center of the old oiled pine floor that allowed heat to come up from the pipeless coal furnace in the basement. One Saturday, we all gathered to watch the movie and Francis "Prig" Berkey dumped a can of black pepper down the grate and onto the top of the furnace. The result was the evacuation of the movie theater and soon after, its demise.

In 1944, St. Pat's Church attempted to keep some of the local boys in line by starting a Boy Scout troop, Troop #37, with Freddie Gonsman taking on the unenviable job as the Scoutmaster. The boys would meet either in the church basement or Freddie's house. We preferred the latter, as his wife Violet would provide us with refreshments. Mrs. Gonsman was a cook at St. Pat's School and a rather stout woman who took no backtalk from anyone. One evening during a Boy Scout meeting at their home, words were exchanged between the two, all in fun. To our delight, Violet suddenly tackled Freddie and wrestled him to the floor…we boys loved it and it was one of the highlights of our time in the troop!

My sister Rita tells me that she and her girlfriends would go to Freddie and Violet's house right after school to watch television. The Gonsman's owned one of the few televisions in town, black and white, of course. The girls would pile into the living room, stretch out on the floor and enjoy a great hour or two of Easy Aces or Mr. Keene - Tracer of Lost Persons, a couple of daytime serials.

The Boy Scout campgrounds were located across Poplar Run and up Sipes Hollow on Puzzletown Road. Our troop went on several camping trips and the memory of one of them still makes me itch! We had set up our tents and built a bonfire, then worked on our merit badges. We went to sleep late every night, and one particular night I was restless and later told that I had been walking in my sleep. Of course, a couple of my "friends" helped me out by walking me around the campground, and I'm sure had a few laughs at my expense.

I awoke the next morning to discover, by way of a lot of itching and redness everywhere (and I mean everywhere!) that they had walked me through a fresh patch of poison ivy. "Dr." Freddie made a feeble attempt to treat the rash, but it had advanced to the point that I needed medical aid. I ended up in the hospital, where I was plastered with medication and wrapped up in bandages like a mummy. Another lesson learned, sleep with one eye open around your buddies!

On another camping trip that took place up the mountain in Kladder, Bill Hite was playing "Tarzan of the Apes" while swinging by a rope from one hill to another and ended up falling into a crevice and breaking his ankle.

I remember my Scouting uniform consisted of an official Boy Scout shirt, neckerchief and hat.

The adventures we had as Boy Scouts always bring back good memories.

Troop #37, 1944. First row-Hezzie, Jay Kagarise, Don Moyer, Boyd Shaw, Don Burk, Pete Cassidy. Second row-Peanuts Billotte, Fred Gonsman (Scoutmaster), Bob Sell, Kent Ritchey, Pat Kelly (flag), Don Trexler, Paul Muri, Bob Lamborn (flag), Joe Hite, Clark George.

Local Girl Scout & Boy Scout Troops, 1947

The early 1940's were a great time to be alive as we Newry boys chased the girls and found new friends to run with. School was tough, as I struggled to learn the ins and outs of basic English. I just couldn't understand the need for dangling participles and the like, but I muddled through and was glad to be leaving grade school behind.

There were fifteen or sixteen kids who graduated from St. Pat's in 1946 and that summer was a fun time. The big war was over, the guys and gals came home safely and life seemed to get back to normal.

Some of our favorite hangouts were W.O. Weimer's poolroom, Langham's Restaurant and "Speed" and Bertie Burk's restaurant beside Benton's house. This was formerly Pete Hite's garage and only a half-block from our house, so it was a great place to loaf. Another

*Mary Alice Gonsman
and Aggie Burk
in front of Pete Hite's garage, 1946*

incentive to spend time at Speed and Bertie's were their three attractive nieces, Mary Lou, Aggie and Janet who came to live in Newry that year. They moved into Mary and Annie Cassidy's house down by St. Pat's Church. What a nice addition to the group of pretty girls already in town!

It was during this period of time when our friends Don and Jim Burk's lives were to take a tragic turn. Their father met an untimely death, and with ten or eleven children in the family, arrangements were made for the girls to go to St. Mary's orphanage in Cresson. The boys were sent to live next door at the St. John's orphanage, and I'm sure this was a very traumatic experience for all the kids.

At the time Don was the only one to stay at home with his mother. I don't recall what prompted the decision, but for some reason this, too, changed and Father Flynn made arrangements for him to go to Boys Town in Nebraska, run by Father Flanagan. I guess we were

Don Burk, 1945

fourteen or fifteen at the time and determined to keep our friend from leaving, so Pete Cassidy and I and a

Don Burk & Hezzie, 1946

couple of other guys decided we would hide Don from Father. Pete had a tent that we took up to Leighty's behind the "Rocks", as the area was known. Our plan was to keep Don there and take turns supplying him with food and keeping him company. Although our plan had a good start, it didn't last long, as sneaking food out of our houses became difficult and we had little money to continue buying supplies. Soon enough our ruse was discovered and Don ended up leaving us. The end result was a good experience for Don as he graduated from Boys Town in 1950. He and I drove out there for a visit in 1952.

While compiling facts for this journal, Elizabeth Black Rhodes was my local historian and provided me with many memories of our Newry childhood. She reminded me of all the swimming holes in the area, like the one at Pap Hite's, Leighty's at the Rocks and Hamil's in Donnertown, a particularly well-known spot. It goes without saying that these swimming holes also served as a place to acquire our Saturday night baths in lieu of the sponge bath variety at home!

Elizabeth's father, Dalton Black, owned a confectionary store located in the upper-half of the McFadden home that boasted of having the first Coke fountain in Newry. Her father was a shrewd businessman, known to lend out money "on interest" and accordingly did very well. As Elizabeth tells it, one Fourth of July he grossed the vast amount of forty dollars, a large part of which, I'm sure, was credit extended.

She also told me that her father and some other people from Newry started a little church called "Gospel Hall."

When I look back on my youth there were only two men in Newry that I was afraid of, Horace Harper and Dalton Black. Elizabeth assures me that her father never would have harmed anyone, but I don't recall ever taking any chances with him! He and Mrs. Dalton kept a very tight "rein" on Elizabeth.

In our teen years, W.O. Weimer was the guy that we would go to for a loan on interest. He always remembered how much you owed him come payday, though I never saw him write anything down.

Back then, trouble seemed to "dog" my brother Paul and I, and the following incident attests to that.

Vince Hart, who lived up the hill from our house, had several large white geese. On our way out to the woods one day, Paul and I decided to "harvest" a few eggs from a goose nest and couldn't wait till we returned home to fry up them up. Apparently we didn't know much about fertilized goose eggs, because when we broke them into one of Mom's cast iron skillets, out came a mess that I can't even begin to describe! For some time after, even chicken eggs made me gag!

Bill Hite relates a time when he and Paul were hanging out behind Pauly Beigle's store and decided to play "scientist" by blowing up some carbide. They put some in a glass jar with water and sealed it, then ran like hell. Nothing happened. When Paul stepped out from behind a wall to check on it, the jar exploded and glass flew. Paul got a deep cut above his eye and blood was spurting everywhere. Bill says he was scared at the sight of all that blood, and though he lived right next door, even more scared of his mother finding out what they had done, so they high-tailed it to our house. My mother stopped the bleeding and dumped some peroxide on the wound, then sent Paul off to see what other fray he could get himself into.

Paul still has a neat scar and should probably consider himself lucky he didn't lose an eye.

An event that was always entertaining and less dangerous (for us anyhow), was watching the airmail "pickup" at the Duncansville airport, now the site of the Puritan clothing plant across from Inlow's.

At one end of the airfield there was a metal frame that looked like a goal post, with a wire attached that held a canvas bag containing the mail. The pilot of the small mail plane would fly over, snatch the bag of mail and lift it up into the plane, while dropping a bag of mail in return. We all enjoyed the show and I remember wondering where all that mail ended up.

There was a small frame hangar located on the grounds of the airfield where Clair Long from Blue

Knob kept a small Piper Cub airplane. One day he took Joe Hite and me up for a ride. What a great experience! I've only flown once since then when Jack Rawlings and I were appraising the City of Altoona Water Works in the late 1960's.

Looking back, it seems that when we weren't out getting into trouble, we were working, and there were always jobs to be had. None of them could be called easy, especially by today's standards, and some were downright nasty. One of those jobs was "shaking hides" and until you have the full description, you really can't appreciate all that it entailed.

When hides were removed from cattle at Shaw's Meat Market, they were covered with rock salt, folded into neat packages and placed in stacks in the hide cellar.

Several times a year when the market price for hides was peaking, Mr. Shaw would hire about six or eight local boys to shake hides alongside the Shaw crew. We would gather early on the appointed day and pull the hides off of the piles in the cellar. Four guys would open them up

Shaw's Meat Market

and lift them over a low wooden frame and shake the rock salt off—thus the name "shaking hides".

The hides were again folded, loaded onto a truck and taken to a railroad car parked by Appleyard's coal yard in Duncansville to be shipped later to a tannery.

Although well paying, this was probably the worst job that we had as kids, back breaking labor for eight to ten hours a day for two or three days. We made a dollar an hour, but most of us hadn't earned that kind of money from the menial jobs we'd done in the past.

We had to dispose of our clothes when the job was done, as hides lying in a cellar for three months emitted an odor that defies description...from shoes to underwear, it was rank!

Bob Moses and I usually worked together, and when we were done for the day, he would head back to Hollidaysburg where he lived. Bob and I were going to the movies one night after work, so we went back to my

house while I cleaned up. Then we went down to the "Diamond" and caught the Blue and White bus to Hollidaysburg. This took place in June or July and the temperature was in

An early Shaw's Delivery Truck

the mid-eighties. Bob was still in his work clothes, head to toe, including shoes.

We made it as far as Sam Thomas' place before Freddie Ironsides, the old bus driver, caught a whiff of Bob's "essence" and stopped the bus to investigate. After quickly assessing the source, he told us in no uncertain terms to exit the bus, which we sheepishly did. I don't believe we even got our fare back!

I guess a farm job that ran a close second to this was when we were hired at Shaw's and Hite's Farms to load bales of hay and straw onto a high wooden wagon pulled by a tractor. Both crops were harvested in late summer during times of extreme heat, and with the chaff blowing off the hay and straw, it was almost unbearable. You'd sweat from the heat and the chaff would stick to your skin and itch like the plague.

Quite a few of us Newryites, guys and girls alike, also worked for a company called the "Green Mountain Cannery" in Martinsburg. We would carpool to the cannery and in teams, head into the huge sweet corn fields to manually pick corn. The corn was then loaded into trucks and hauled back to the cannery. This job started very early in the morning when the dew hung heavy on the cornstalks, and we were usually wet from head to toe until the sun came out, then we sweltered in the heat.

Today these jobs would be considered bonded slavery and probably illegal for kids our age, but back then the money was good and we always needed school clothes...not to mention, allowances were unheard of in the Thompson household!

Another fellow who would hire us was a kindly gentleman, Russell Burket, who had a farm out beyond Shaw's. There was an old dug well on the property that was lined to its full depth with large stones. Evidently some type of algae had developed on the interior of the well, so Mr. Burket devised a plan to eliminate the problem.

The well was drained and a ladder was lowered to the bottom so we could scrape the walls. I know when I descended the ladder into the pit, I wasn't a happy employee and I let Mr. Burket know it!

Somehow he convinced us to complete the job and we stayed until all that green, foul-smelling gunk was gone. Only then were we allowed to exit that "hell hole". Another of those long remembered jobs of my youth!

Early in my career as a day laborer, several of us were hired by Father Smith, I believe the rector at St. Bernadine's Monastery.

At the time, Pat Bradley's father operated the farm on the property and had a herd of cattle that provided milk and meat for the seminarians who lived there.

Our job was to hoe long rows of corn that were planted parallel to the river and stretched from Catfish Road to the Long Hole. Those rows were probably quarter of a mile in length, so we would hoe one down and one back and repeat this back-breaking task until quitting time, usually about six o'clock in the evening. The job lasted until the corn grew higher than the weeds, then Father would find something else for his "peasant workers" to do. The pay for this labor was I'm sure minimal, as the Franciscan friars were not known for their generosity!

A side note – during the course of this job, the boys discovered the wine cellar in the friary basement where wine was bottled for use by the Franciscans in the area. We managed to sample the "product" off and on until one day when the boss, Father Smith, caught us in the act and literally booted us off the grounds.

Worse, he told us that he was going to inform our parents of our sinful behavior! After giving me a verbal reaming (I'm sure just to please the good friar), my dad told me later that I should have brought home some of the vintage. Being that Dad's father produced "white lightning" up the mountain and peddled it out of his old 1930 Ford, my dad knew vintage!

Speaking of "moonshine", I remember my mom telling a story about Dad and his brother Walter, also known as "Tillie", hauling moonshine down from Lilly and Portage where their stills were hidden. Dad was driving when the "Revenooers" (I guess the State Police) spotted them. Dad and Tillie attempted to outrun the law but their truck overturned and they were both thrown out.

Uncles Walter (Tillie) and Regis Thompson Dad's brothers

Dad was rendered unconscious and when he came to, he couldn't find Tillie, so he raced home. Bolting in the back door, he yelled to my mother, "Pack my clothes! I have to get out of town, I think I just killed Tillie!"

The rest of the story is vague, but apparently after the accident, Tillie saw Dad laying there and thought he was dead, so he left and walked home. I never heard what happened after that, but I'm sure it was only one of the many adventures in my Dad's life, being one in a family of five ornery boys.

Tillie was always known for finding a way to "make a buck". Shortly before Thanksgiving one year, he and a couple of his friends found out about a turkey farm in the area ripe for the picking. They proceeded to "borrow" several turkeys and went around Newry selling them. Bill Hite told me that his mom, believing Tillie owned the turkeys, bought one for their holiday dinner. I'm not sure that the turkey salesmen were ever caught!

When I was growing up, Dad's family held a reunion every year at our Uncle Pat's in Ore Hill. The highlight for us kids was a ride in the hay wagon pulled

Uncle Tillie

by an old tractor. I remember when Dad and his brothers would get into the strong liquor, the women would take over the festivities. Uncle Pat's wife, Sarah, was truly a saint, like all of the Thompson wives. I guess this still stands true a generation later, as my brothers and I have tended to stretch the "marital bliss" a bit...hopefully there is an all-forgiving God who will understand when the time comes!

We continue the tradition of the Thompson family reunion and gather together once a year at Lakemont Park. It's always great to see everyone and catch up on each other's lives. My kids have said we should sell

Thompson family reunion 1940. Dad holding me, Mom holding Paul,
Phitty holding Babe (notice the dress he's wearing!)
and Ray in the front covering his face.

admission tickets to the public, because no one would
believe some of the stories told when my brothers and I
get together. What a bunch of characters!

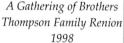

A Gathering of Brothers
Thompson Family Renion
1998

Like us boys, "trouble" seemed to follow my dad.
(Although after recounting some of the stories in this
journal, I'm starting to think that the problem wasn't as
much us as it was the "bad influences" we hung around
with!)

This next incident supplied the Newry boys with a

Dad and boys. Bottom row-Babe, Terry Thompson
(Ray's son), Dad, Raymond, Hezzie.
Top row-Butch, Jim, Paul, Dewey.

laugh for quite a while.

Dad and Shell Hite usually made the Wonder Bar their Saturday night "watering hole" and their preferred mode of transportation was Shell's small model something Ford pickup truck. One Saturday night after Shell and my dad were firmly ensconced at the bar,

Dad and I, 1978

several of the local boys, my brother Jake among them, came up with a great stunt. They lifted Shell's old pickup truck and positioned it between a telephone pole and Tommy

George's house ...sideways.

When Shell and Dad finally exited the Wonder Bar in the wee hours of the morning, they couldn't believe their eyes! My dad was to have said, "How the hell did you ever park that truck there, Shell?"

I'm not sure how they got home that night, but that gag went down in history as one of the better ones. I can just imagine the comments by the Sunday churchgoers when they passed that truck the next morning!

Occasionally, Dad would walk home from a night on the town, needless to say, a bit unsteady on his feet. Every now and then he would take a fall and end up losing his dentures. As he went out on Saturday nights and refused to go to Sunday Mass without his "teeth", we boys would be awakened at daybreak to go in search of them...we usually found them down by the bridge at Duck Creek.

As much as I hate to admit it, I believe that some of my dad's traits may have rubbed off on a few of my brothers — Jake and Ray especially!

In 1945 an extraordinary event occurred in our house – the birth of a baby girl! After seven boys in a row, Mom was overjoyed when our sister Rita came along. Somehow Rita became "Honey", a cute little blonde with kinky hair and a dimpled smile. Even the girls in Newry weren't immune to acquiring a nickname!

Due to the lack of available space, baby Rita slept in a big wooden crib in the upstairs hallway until she was a toddler. I imagine it was thought by a couple of her brothers that she was only "temporary" and didn't need a room of her own!

Our dad made "home brew" and root beer and used the big unfinished attic to store these concoctions while they were "working". This attic was located right above Rita's hallway bedroom. As the weather turned warm, the surface of the old tin roof would heat up to one-hundred plus degrees and cause the bottle lids on the brew to "pop". Rita says this usually happened through the night and scared the daylights out of her!

Top left-Dad and our little Honey, 1948.
Top right-Mom and her long-awaited girl, 1946.
Lower left-Rita, 1946. Lower right-Rita, 1948.

Babe and Rita, 1948

Babe, as a little guy, was a tad spoiled and was known for "playing dead". If he didn't get his own way, he would drop where he was and lay there. We learned just to step over him and ignore him, and after a while he would "come alive" again. We still remind him of this stunt when we get together, a fact I'm sure he doesn't appreciate!

114

What a crew!
First row-Babe, Honey, Dewey.
Second row-Joe, Popeye, Jim. Middle-Butch.

Every family history should include a chapter on pets and ours is no exception. Along with kids, there were always plenty of animals at our house, mostly dogs of various breeds who called our back porch home. There were mutts, beagles and cocker spaniels of all colors, in addition to a few cats. With the help of my sisters Phyllis and Rita, we were able to recall a few of the names—Buffy, Inky, Ginger, Rusty, Cappy and Toodles, along with some who weren't even with us long enough to be named. I'm sure the fact that we lived along old Route 220 lessened the life expectancies of many of the animals! We also had Belgian rabbits with long droopy ears that we got from P.Z. Imler's, a variety of short-eared rabbits, and a memorable one that only had three legs…memorable because one day it went missing and the meat dish for the next day's dinner looked awfully suspicious!

Over the years we acquired some "not so common" pets too, thanks to my brothers, who delighted in bringing them home for the rest of us to enjoy. My wife Charleen remembers my mother telling her of the time she had just finished making a huge pot of bean soup for dinner when a couple of my brothers came in to the kitchen to show off their new pet. My mom turned from the stove to see a large snake slithering across her kitchen floor...but wait, it gets better! One of the boys had come over to show her the grasshopper he had found, and you guessed it, that grasshopper hopped right into the big pot of bean soup! The snake turned out to be just one of many who made a home with our family. I don't believe we ever found out what became of the grasshopper!

My sister Phyllis reminded me of the time my brothers and I found a large black snake and brought it home. Curious boys that we were, we dissected it and were excited to find a bunch of little baby snakes inside...which according to Phyllis we proceeded to hang on my mother's clothesline to surprise her the next time she hung out laundry!

In his youth, our brother Ray acquired the dubious skill of being able to "desensitize" a skunk. So we also had quite a few of this breed walking about our house. Of course, they would scare the heck out of visitors, which always provided us with a chuckle. I believe Ray even sold a few of these altered creatures to other families, but I'm sure they weren't as well-received as they were in our home.

Over the years, several raccoons also joined our family and took up residence under a couch or a cupboard. Mom didn't appreciate them as tenants, as their favorite pastime was chewing on her living room curtains. When the curtains became too chewed up to keep, she would give them to Rita and her friends, who cut them up and fashioned new clothes for their dolls. It didn't take much to make my mother happy, so when she was able to purchase new curtains, she thought she was rich!

Rounding out our menagerie was our pet rat, "Whitey", who slept in a shoe box under the couch. Phyllis' boyfriend Jessie, later her husband, was visiting one evening when Whitey decided to pop out to say hello. He crawled up the couch and over the back of Jessie's neck. Let's just say that Jessie was not as happy to make his acquaintance!

My friend, Pete Cassidy, had a "talking" crow who really could mouth a few guttural words. It was said that someone split the crow's tongue and taught it to talk, but this story may have just been one of the "good ones" passed around the local watering holes.

Can you imagine my mother with all those kids and a whole slew of critters? You can see why as adults, my brothers and sisters and I refer to her as a "saint"…she really did put up with a lot.

Babe with Rusty & Inky, 1949

Butch, Ginger and the
"one that didnt get away", 1950

THE TEEN YEARS

Good Buddies! Pat Kelly, Pete Cassidy, Hezzie, 1950

I consider September of 1946 to be my initiation into the "real world" as the change from our little class of fifteen eighth graders to a couple hundred ninth graders at Hollidaysburg Junior High was quite an adjustment for me. I learned to cope with changing classes and riding a school bus along with what I thought was way too much homework.

My freshman year at the junior high on the hill was not without incident, of course. Being a country boy, I had the habit of checking out any and all snakes that crossed my path. One day during the school year, I found a cute little garter snake and put it in a matchbox. Somehow that box ended up on top of my desk in Biology class and one of the girls opened it and saw the snake. This, of course, disrupted the whole class, so my teacher, Miss Ramsey, sent my little "friend" and I down the hall to see Mr. Loree, the Principal. Surprisingly, he wasn't impressed with my snake either and the resulting punishment didn't bode well for my grade in deportment!

Junior high school introduced me to some of the finest teachers I've ever had the pleasure of knowing. As I've indicated earlier in this journal, my talents in English were limited, but I gained new insights into the intricacies of the English language through the wisdom of my English teacher, Miss Eudora Meyers. Miss Meyers was a slender lady, very prim and proper, and left little doubt that she was the one in authority and you were the one being taught!

During the course of the school year, one of our assignments was to write an autobiography. Now, I couldn't spell the word, let alone write one, but after Miss Meyers explained the format, I began. I thought I had done a fairly good job when I had finished the assignment, but Miss Meyers disagreed. She took me aside and very nicely asked me to "edit" mine before presenting it to the class. I was a little hurt, in that I had merely written of the particulars of growing up in the country with eleven brothers and sisters. Granted, I may have been a tad too descriptive with certain details pertaining to our various outhouses, sleeping three brothers to a bed or the birthing of one or more of my brothers at home with the assistance of the local midwife. But, being a conscientious student, I accepted the criticism of the one whose desk occupied a more prominent position than mine, and again struggled through the assignment of writing my life story. I suppose you could call that an attempt at "cleaning up my act." I believe my grade for this cleansing ended up being a 90%!

Thank goodness for a Eudora Meyers at that time of my life. To this day she spends her ninety plus years in reasonably good health and we remain close friends.

Another great teacher from my freshman year was my Math teacher, Mr. Raymond Lamberson, who was known for being a tough coach and a real gentleman. He, like Miss Meyers, let you know right up front who was boss!

An early baseball team. Players included Homer Glunt, Charles Lykens, John Bogel, Tom McCoy, Simon Weaver, Frank Weaver, Tom Weaver, Warren McCoy.

It seemed that we were living high in the late 1940's, what with sports, girls and fun times. Although the war years had somewhat derailed the sport of baseball in Newry and other small towns in Blair and Cambria Counties, it brought about the advent of the "Catholic League." Several Catholic churches, including St. Pat's, fielded teams made up of some of the local teenage boys.

Fred Gonsman, our old Boy Scout leader, was our manager and coach and provided transportation to away games. As I was not known for my speed, Fred decided to make me a pitcher. He thought my being a "leftie" would give me an edge since most of the batters were "righties".

"Strategy Meeting?"
Jim Stalter, Jack "Skip" Beegle, Clark George
1948

While I don't recall much spring training, I'll never forget my first outing. My catcher had his work cut out for him as my record for the one inning I pitched consisted of five walks and three hit batsman! I begged Fred to release me and he gladly conceded. That ended my dream of ever playing in the big leagues!

Baseball continued to grow in popularity after the war. The Blair County League and the Blair Twilight League was formed, the latter name befitting as most of their games were played in the evening after a full day's work. For sure many a game was replayed in Piney McCoy's tavern and the Wonder Bar.

Although space doesn't permit all the records and names of the many stars that played on county ball fields, I've chosen a few photos for the end of this book that account the history of some of these baseball heroes.

A sport enjoyed by all was boxing. It was a rite of passage for the local young men, though oft times brutal. Scrappy Weaver reminded me of an unfortunate accident involving his brother Wayne. The boys in town had a makeshift boxing ring located in Mr. Black's garage and one night my dad's brother Tillie and Wayne were boxing. Tillie knocked Wayne out, which evidently caused a brain aneurism that resulted in Wayne's death. Truly a terrible accident and thus ended the boxing events in our little town.

Back in the days of World War II, the older guys who didn't enjoy baseball or boxing created their own entertainment, consisting of an outdoor "casino" located under a big oak tree at one end of the Newry ballfield. The younger kids could make forty or fifty cents a day just by managing the cold water concession. I remember hearing that a local boy, Peany Diehl, was home on leave from the Army one weekend and joined the boys for a game or two. He ended up going back to camp with a whole pocket full of money! One of the perks of serving in the armed forces was that you usually came out a much better card player!

My dad was known for hosting quite a few card games in the parlor of our house during inclement weather, but the accommodations didn't come free, as Mr. T. would "rake" a quarter from each game as host!

We boys inherited a bit of the gambling gene and held our own poker games, although we played for matches. We would buy nickel boxes of wooden matches, a hundred to a box and divvy them up among the players. Our poker games would take place on one of the big metal beds on the second floor of our house. One night Joe Hite, Don Burk and I, along with a couple of other guys, were in the midst of a serious game when Joe announced it was time for him to go home. He started down the steps that led to the center hall and met up with my dad, who was standing there talking to a neighbor, Ike Diehl. As Joe passed them he said, "Excuse me, Mr. Thompson." Dad, without even looking his way, picked Joe up by the seat of his pants and said, "You get the hell back up those steps, where the hell do you think you're going?" Joe, not wanting to challenge him, high-tailed it back up the steps to tell us that our dad wouldn't let him leave.

We ended up taking Joe over to Phyllis' bedroom where we opened a window that overlooked the back

Joe Hite & Hezzie

porch and dropped him down the side of the house to the ground! I guess when you had nine boys running around like my dad did, you didn't bother looking at faces, you just told them where to go! Joe Hite and I still laugh about that episode.

Sometimes, after throwing together enough money for gas, a bunch of us guys would go down to Pat Kelly's to cajole him into taking us for a ride in his 1936 Ford.

Often Pat's dad, Pius, would meet us at the back door and inform us that their family was saying the Rosary. Pointing his finger, he would bark "Get the hell

Pat Kelly, 1950

in there and kneel down, we're _all_ saying the Rosary!"

Although this was a daily ritual in the Kelly household, there were those in our group who weren't Catholic and had no clue what a Rosary was.

Believe me, they learned quickly or soon found out there would be no "joyride" forthcoming!

My friends and I were approaching high school about this time and gaining interest in cars and motorcycles. The lucky guys who could afford them would drive to school and it was a big deal to pull up in

Hezzie on Jake's Motorcycle, 1948

Looking Sharp, Hezzie!

125

your 1936 Ford or 1939 Chevrolet. I believe gasoline back then was six gallons for ninety-nine cents at Johnny McCoy's gas station!

I couldn't afford my own car and my dad wasn't about to sign for me, but I was able to buy into a 1939 Chevy with Joe Hite. Our partnership dissolved some time later, more than likely because the car needed tires, which were five dollars each, used, and a twelve-dollar battery. It was great while it lasted though!

In those days Pete Cassidy had a small motorized cycle, something on the order of a moped. I managed to hitch a ride with him often; the top speed of the cycle was around twenty-five miles an hour, but it got us where we were going.

Pete Cassidy 1948

A favorite hangout of ours was Vi and Willard Inlow's hot dog stand in Duncansville, next to the Aviation Inn. This little building, established in 1948, was about thirty feet long and twenty feet wide and its claim to fame was the famous twelve-inch hot dog. There were only six or eight stools at the counter along with a little sit-down area, but the atmosphere along with the smell of hot dogs grilling and onions steaming, helped make Inlow's a special spot. If I recall correctly, you could purchase three hot dogs for a dollar!

Amazingly, Inlow's is still going strong and serving up those delicious hot dogs to this day.

Inlow's, 1950.
Phyllis and I owned the 1940 Plymouth in the foreground.

Inlow's Famous Foot-Longs

*Pete Cassidy and
Joe Thompson,
Pete's 1949 Ford*

*Hezzie,
praying for redepmtion?
1946*

*Popeye
1948*

*Hezzie, Joe, and Popeye
1950*

Late 1940's
Looking Snazzy, Hezzie!

Hezzie, 1952

Paul and Hezzie 1952

Marcella Muri and Mary Kelly
In front of
Speed and Bertie's Restaurant

Hezzie and Floyd Burket

Floyd Burket, Pete Cassidy, Hezzie, Tappy, Popeye

During the school year, most of the kids hung out at the Sugar Bowl, also known as "Pete the Greek's" and enjoyed their famous Chocolate Frost and root beer floats.

The Sugar Bowl

Blue & White Snack Bar

Closer to the high school was the Blue and White Snack Bar, opened in 1949 by "Curly" Kerns. Still in existence today, this small shop fed many a student who couldn't stomach the institutional cafeteria food.

When we all pooled our spare change and could put a couple of bucks worth of gas together we'd make the trip to Taylor's Drive-In or one of the other eating establishments on Pleasant Valley Boulevard in the "big city" of Altoona.

We were young kids with little money and lots of time…but boy, what a time we had!

During my years at Hollidaysburg Junior High School and Hollidaysburg Area High School, I established friendships that have endured to the present day and look forward to seeing everyone at our reunions. My classmates and I recently celebrated our 60th Senior Class Reunion in 2010. How time flies!

Hezzie
1950

MY MOTHER

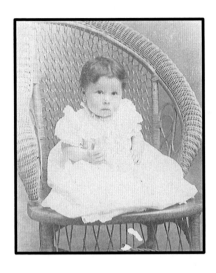

These writings would not be complete if I failed to include a few words about my mother, Edith Evangeline Leonard Thompson. As I have stated previously in this journal, my brothers and sisters and I have always considered my mother to be a wise and saintly woman who lived for nothing more than to care for her family.

Baking was just one of Mom's many talents and she could whip up a delicious cake at a moment's notice, or bake enough pies, usually four or five at a time, to feed her troops.

My sister Rita tells me that she was Mom's little helper when she made her wonderful homemade bread, baked from her own recipe. As Mom finished kneading each of the ten or twelve loaves she would make at a time and put them in their individual pans,

Rita would carry them to the hall stairs leading up to the second floor and set each pan on the edge of a step, where the heat from the furnace would cause the dough to rise. Once sufficiently risen, the dough would then be placed in our big stove. Believe me, my brothers and I (and many of our friends) always looked forward to coming home to a slice or two of Mom's bread.

Mom told me once that she loved to fish when she was young, and that she and her dad would catch the early morning train to Petersburg. Having packed an "all-day" lunch, they would sit along the Petersburg branch of the Juniata River and fish, then catch the train home in the evening.

My mother loved to Christmas shop for everyone, so a month before Christmas she would sit down and make her list, usually four or five pages filled with the names of her twelve children, their spouses, the numerous grandchildren, aunts and uncles, neighborhood children and anyone else who came to mind. A fair estimate would be around eighty names.

Because Mom didn't drive, she would enlist one of us to take her to H. L. Green's or Murphy's in Hollidaysburg, or Tri-State and Gables in Altoona. If you were the designated driver, you knew you were in for a three or four hour trip! Her dedication to making the holiday special was legendary.

When she was unable to make the trip herself, she would delegate the chore to several of her kids, who gladly obliged. In her later years she would send out a card with a (freshly ironed!) dollar bill to all. I still remember receiving her card containing a crisp dollar bill when I was in my mid-forties!

I could fill many more pages with my mother's loving gestures, but suffice it to say that all of the Newry kids wanted our Mom to be their Mom, and to many, she was.

Mom, 1967

When I started this journal in 1999, I envisioned sharing the happenings of my life and the lives of others who have meant so much to me growing up in our little town of Newry, Pennsylvania.

My journey has become so much more. I've come to realize through my writings that I am truly blessed...blessed to have had the experiences I've written about, good and bad, blessed that I've had the pleasure of meeting the most wonderful people and the opportunity to forge many long lasting friendships. You, my friends, have helped make me the man I am today, and I thank all of you who became part of my life.

I hope that you have enjoyed reliving these memories as much as I have sharing them with you,

Hezzie

*Grandpap
and
Grandma Thompson*

*Great Grandpap DeLozier,
My Mother's Grandpap*

Newry—Do you remember the following news items recorded in Newry April 16, 1919: These spring days and evenings have once again brought out some few girls and boys who insist on kissing at the gate. One lassie answered the beef through a local newspaper declaring, "Why should the newspaper reporter beef off because of kissing at the gate when my mother and father do not disapprove?" The editor added "Maybe your parents would like to be relieved of the financial responsibility of keeping you." . . . Miss Lulu Holland, assistant to the Newry postmaster, was spending a vacation in Pittsburgh. . . . Newry in the yesteryear boasted of three top-ranking blacksmith shops, but this date found the last one going out of business, due to the presence of automobiles.

Altoona Mirror Columns
by
Mary D. Shaw

Newry Is Still Noisy.

EDITOR of the Altoona Mirror —In answer to the letter recently published in this paper, I would like to bring out to the citizens of Newry a few points of interest.

At 3 o'clock on a recent Saturday morning an exhibition of dare deviltry was carried on, but the party who wrote that letter to the Mirror did not mention how, in previous years and today the same thing is being done in this small town, only by different parties.

Why then was this not before the citizens? I personally agree that something should be done about this recent exhibition. But why should we hit only the motorcycles and let the cars go through town like mad with their musical horns and at any hour of the morning.

This is anything but pleasure and I think something should be done about this situation.

A CITIZEN OF NEWRY.

Roaring Spring—Were you one of the following young people of Roaring Spring, who on the evening of July 16, 1915, were guests at a party given in the home of Mr. and Mrs. Charles Thompson, a popular young couple who operated a farm in the area? Mr. and Mrs. John Thompson, Mrs. Eliza Thompson, Gerals Moses, Mary O'Neil, Mrs. F. D. Eger, Mrs. Aaron Diehl, Mrs. Annie Baker, Margaret Thompson, Stella and Blanche Ritchey, Marie Treml, Mary Diehl, Gertie Thompson, Ella Eger, Marie Shaw, Edna Moyer, Olene Baker, Helen Diehl, Gerald, Eugene and Lester Walter, Regis Thompson, Ward Charles, Regis and Robert Diehl, George and Leo Lanzendorfer, Malcom and Charles Ritchey, James and Michael Diehl, Ward Wilt, Charles Snowberger, Clarence Long and Alvin Shaw.

It is really something to remember our thrilling Saturday nights. You were always so clean it was disgusting. You were allowed to walk to town and buy a dish of ice cream, walk back home and go to bed at 10 p.m. If you had weeded and hoed the garden, cut stove wood, fed the chickens, and cut the grass with a sickle, then you were allowed to take a walk on Sunday afternoon. There were no movies, no funny books, no automobiles, no scooters and few bicycles, cigarets were unknown by the kids; you did smoke some corn-silk and got sick; dad smoked few cigars, but the old corncob pipe was clicking 12 hours of the day. You were allowed to have your friends in the kitchen, you could edge now and then into the living room, but, brother, you could have broken into a bank much easier than to edge into the parlor. Would you like to live some of those days again?

137

Olden Wash Days.

WOMEN TODAY, whose most difficult washday chore may be getting the soap carton open, can get some idea of how far things have improved since great-grandma's day from the following item out of the past.

It's an authentic Kentucky "receipt," in its original spelling, for washing clothes, contributed by a reader to the Colorado Interstate Gas Co. magazine:

1. bild a fire in back yard to heet kettle of rain water.

2. set tubs so smoke won't blow in eyes if wind is pert.

3. shave one hole cake soap in bilin water.

4. sort things, make three piles. 1 pile white, 1 pile cullord. 1 pile work britches and rags.

5. stur flour in cold water to smooth then thin down with bilin water.

6. rub dirty spots on board, scrub hard. then bile. rub cullord but don't bile—just rench and starch.

7. take white things out of kettle with broom stick handle then rench, blew and starch.

8. spred tee towels on grass.

9. hang old rags on fence.

10. pore rench water in flower bed.

11. scrub porch with hot soapy water.

12. turn tubs upside down.

13. go put on cleen dress—smooth hair with side combs—brew cup of tee—set and rest and rock a spell and count blessins.

Mothers of today, those deep in laundry work, surely can count their "blessings" quite differently.

Altoona Mirror columns by Mary D. Shaw

Newry—Do you remember back to the afternoon and evening of March 1, 1924, when the students of St. Patrick's school enjoyed a sledding party from Newry to Butlerville? Sisters Genevieve and Corsilia were in charge of the party while the big horse-drawn sleds were under the direction of Harold Holland, Ralph Hite, Chalmer Smith and Henry Glass. Those in the party included: Elizabeth Hoover, Anna Boyles, Helen Moses, Mary Weyant, Madelene Hoover, Evelyn Sell, Helen Hodge, Madeline Hite, Jennie Bogle, Marie Eger, Catherine Weaver, Gertrude George, Jessie Hines, Arthur Hoover, Gerald Moses, Harold Hines, Ralph Yingling, Oliver Thompson, Charles McCormick, Lester Yingling, Robert Zeith, Lloyd Moyer, Paul Weaver, Raymond Weyandt, Androcas Hoover, Rosemary Hite, Imelda Doll, Grace Bogle, Theodore Hite, Nellie Weaver, Beatrice Moses, Mollie Hoover, Mary Yingling, Orlean Harker, Geraldine Conrad, Margaret Harker, Paul Conrad, Bernard Weaver, Francis Burke, Roger McDonnell, Joseph Hoover, Raymond Eger, Dean Harker, Michael Montgomery and Leo Moyer.

An early wedding picture in front of the Buckel House

The Buckel House, now the home of the Wonder Bar

The old hitching rail on the Diamond

Early Transportation!

Local boys from the 30's
Sammy Eller,
Paul Burk,
Tom Montgomery

St. Pat's Church
Built in 1816 and removed in 2007-2008.
(A new church was erected and dedicated in 2008)

Inside old St. Pat's Church

Early residents hitchin' a ride
on old Rte. 220

William Buckel's blacksmith shop, Bedford Street.
Left to right - unknown, William Buckel, Grant Hall, Dalton Black, unknown

Very early photos of The Bogel House
It still stands today and is reported to be the oldest house in Newry

Newry Public School Class of 1925, Mary D. Shaw, teacher

Newry Public School Class of 1938. First row-Leona Burkey, Edie Burkey, Orpha Helsel, Doris Long, Stiffler, Iris Shaw, Betty Conrad, Clete Peck, Gene Paul Cassidy, Boyd Shaw, Mary Beigle, Eunice Burkey. Second row-Mary Wilt, teacher, Adelaide Long, Yvonne Conrad, Betty Beigle, Edna Peck, Marion Shaw, Bob Beigle, Shirley Burkey, Joann Long, AnnaMae Fissell. Third row-Gertrude Spidle, Phyllis Burkey, Ruth Thompson, Francis Burkey, Loris Glunt, Pat Cassidy, George Benton, Jim Malone, Scrappy Weaver. Fourth row-Maggie McFadden, Virginia Glunt, Elizbeth Black, Gerald Bogel, Conwell Glunt, Bill Beigle, Eldon Shaw, Frank Teeter, teacher.

*Newry Public School Class of 1948. First row-Donald Riling, Ronald Riling,
Garry Weaver, Richard Shaw, James McCoy, Dalton Hite, Pepsi Thompson,
Donald Shaw, George Burket, Donna McFadden, Beverly Berkey, Gloria Peck,
Helen Mae McFadden, Ronald Smith. Second row-Wayne Conrad, Richard
Peck, George Glass, Henry Burkett, Robert Lamborn, Mrs. Wilt, teacher, Gary
Hite, John Fissel, Mary Benton, Donna Kagarise, Donald Leighty.*

*St. Pat's-An eighth grade graduation class. First row-Dolores Kelly,
Denise Gonsman, Janet Burk, Joan Bradley, Ann Sell, Sister
Philomena, Paul Thompson, George Biesinger, William Culp, Donald
Noel, Colleen Dodson. Second row-Amelia Harker, Edna Zeth, William
Hite, Charles Wilt, Lois Hite, Bob Zeth.*

Newry Baseball Team 1940. First row- Paul Weaver, Ted Long, Tom Weaver (bat boy). Second row-Bob Conrad, Pat George, Francis Weaver, Wilfrid Benton, William Conrad, Bob Hite. Third row-Paul Weaver (manager), Rodney Conrad, Ferd Hite, John Culp, Charles Conrad, W.O. Wimer

Newry Baseball Team, Blair Twilight League, 1948 Champions. First row-bat boys Joe Dodson, Joe Thompson. Second row-Jim Malone, Scrappy Weaver, John McCoy, Jim Stalter, Jess Conrad, Bob Conrad, Jack Beegle. Third row-Clark George, Abie Link, Rodney Conrad, Whitey Conrad, Sam Moses, Candy Thompson. Third row-Fred Gonsman, Glenn Conrad, Paul Weaver, Kent Ritchey, Bruce Ritchey, Floyd Burket, S. Fissel. Back-W.O. Weimer

Newry Baseball Team 1951. First row-Wayne Conrad, Palmer Loose, Pete Cassidy, John Weaver (batboy), Lefty Brubaker, Rod Hite. Second row-Kent Ritchey, H. Hileman, Joe Hite, C. Evans. Third row-John McCoy, Scrappy Weaver, Marion Brantner, Clyde Piper, Paul Weaver, manager

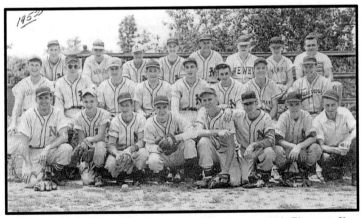

Newry Baseball Team, Blair County Twilight League, 1952. First row-Jim Malone, Don Zeth, Floyd Burket, George Glass, Carl Evans, Cliff Burket, Joe Thompson, Fred Gonsman. Second row-Cletus Thompson, Jack Beegle, Tom Weaver, Lou Lanzendorfer, Paul Muri, Pete Cassidy, Buck Thomas, Robinson. Third row-Kent Ritchey, Dick Fleck, Dwayne Eicher, Wayne Conrad, Joe Hite, Lou Keller, John Zeth, Pat Cassidy

Newry Baseball Team 1953. First row-Scrappy Weaver, Pete Cassidy, Wayne Conrad, Don Zeth, Ned Whetstone, Clyde Piper. Second row-Paul Weaver (manager), George Glass, Lou Muri, John McCoy, Bill Hite, Jack Beegle, Gene Wentz, Carl Evans, Jim Malone, Don Booth

Newry Blair Twilight Team 1954. First row-Fred Weaver, Pete Cassidy, Paul Weaver, Wayne Conrad, John McCoy, George Glass. Second row-Paul Weaver (manager), Art Walker, Tim Crawford, Jim Wentz, Bill Hite, Gene Showalter, Dick Peck, Jim Malone

Newry Baseball Team 1957. First row-Scrappy Weaver, John McCoy, Clyde Piper, George Glass, Wayne Conrad. Second row-Dick Shaw, Ron Coho, Musser, Don Zeth, Earl Hite, Bill Hite

Joe, bat boy 1949

Hobo / TrampSigns

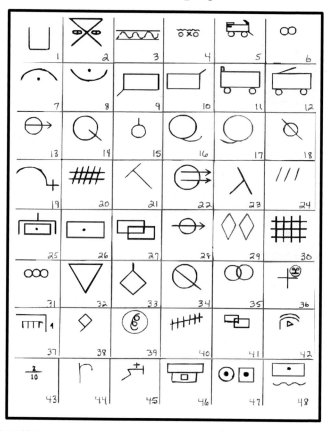

1. Camp Here
2. Safe Camp
3. Bad Water
4. Good Water
5. Catch Out Here
6. Don't Give Up
7. Cops Active
8. Cops Inactive
9. No Alcohol Town
10. Town Allows Alcohol
11. Railroad
12. Trolley
13. Go
14. At Crossroad
    Go this Way
15. Straight Ahead
16. Turn Right Here
17. Turn Left Here
18. Good Road to Follow
19. Stop
20. Unsafe Place
21. Get Out Fast
22. Get Out Fast
23. Keep Away
24. Unsafe Area
25. Dangerous
    Neighborhood
26. Danger
27. Afraid
28. Don't Go this Way
29. Be Quiet
30. Jail (yeggs)
31. Chain Gang
32. Tramps Here
33. Be Ready to
    Defend Yourself
34. Worth Robbing (yeggs)
35. Hoboes Arrested on Sight
36. Doctor No Charge
37. Beware! 4 Dogs
38. Hold Your Tongue
39. Courthouse or
    Police Station
40. You'll get Cursed Out Here
41. Cowards! Will give
    to get rid of you
42. You can sleep in the loft
43. There are crooks around
44. Care here if you are sick
45. Food for Working
46. Well Guarded Home
47. Bad Tempered Man Here
48. Dangerous Drinking Water

Hobo / TrampSigns

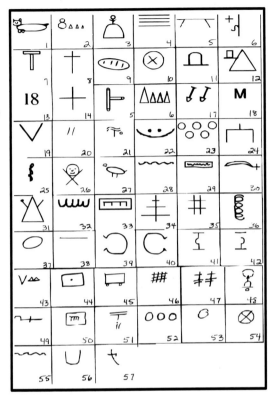

1. Kindhearted Lady
2. Kind Woman
3. Woman
4. Housewife Feed for Chores
5. Sit Down Feed
6. Food for Work
7. Food for Working
8. Talk Religion Get Food
9. Bread
10. Good for a Handout
11. Gentlemen
12. Wealthy
13. I ate
14. Alright (ok)
15. Easy Mark
16. Tell Pitiful Story
17. Work Available
18. Tell Hard Luck Story Here
19. Fake Illness Here
20. Anything Goes
21. Sleep in Barn
22. Can Sleep in Barn
23. Good Chance to Get Money Here
24. Here is the Place
25. Help if Sick
26. Doctor
27. Telephone
28. Poor Man
29. Bad Tempered Owner
30. Dishonest Man
31. Man with a Gun
32. Dog
33. Bad Dog
34. Officer
35. Police Officer Lives Here
36. Judge
37. Nothing Doing Here
38. Doubtful
39. Owner Home
40. Owner Out
41. No One Home
42. Someone Home
43. 2 Women Here Tell Good Story
44. Danger! Brutal Man
45. Get Carfare Here
46. A Crime has been done here
47. Danger
48. Woman Living Alone
49. A Fence Lives Here
50. Dog in the Garden
51. May Sleep in the Hayloft
52. May Get Money Here
53. Nothing Doing Here
54. Ok Here, Good chance for Food
55. Poor People
56. May Sleep Here
57. Policewomen Lives Here

Hobo lingo in use up to the 1940s

- Accommodation car - The caboose of a train
- Angellina - young inexperienced kid
- Bad Road - A train line rendered useless by some hobo's bad action
- Banjo - (1) A small portable frying pan. (2) A short, "D" handled shovel.
- Barnacle - a person who sticks to one job a year or more
- Beachcomber - a hobo who hangs around docks or seaports.
- Big House - Prison
- Bindle stick - Collection of belongings wrapped in cloth and tied around a stick
- Bindlestiff - A hobo who steals from other hobos.
- Blowed-in-the-glass - a genuine, trustworthy individual
- "'Bo" - the common way one hobo referred to another: "I met that 'Bo on the way to Bangor last spring".
- Boil Up - Specifically, to boil one's clothes to kill lice and their eggs. Generally, to get oneself as clean as possible
- Bone polisher - A mean dog.
- Bone orchard - a graveyard
- Bull - A railroad officer
- Bullets - Beans
- Buck - a Catholic priest good for a dollar
- Buger - Today's lunch
- C, H, and D - indicates an individual is Cold, Hungry, and Dry (thirsty)
- California Blankets - Newspapers, intended to be used for bedding
- Calling In - Using another's campfire to warm up or cook
- Cannonball - A fast train
- Carrying the Banner - Keeping in constant motion so as to avoid being picked up for loitering or to keep from freezing
- Catch the Westbound - to die
- Chuck a dummy - Pretend to faint
- Cover with the moon - Sleep out in the open
- Cow crate - A railroad stock car
- Crumbs - Lice
- Doggin' it - Traveling by bus, especially on the Greyhound bus line
- Easy mark - A hobo sign or mark that identifies a person or place where one can get food and a place to stay overnight
- Elevated - under the influence of drugs or alcohol
- Flip - to board a moving train
- Flop - a place to sleep, by extension: "Flophouse", a cheap hotel.

- Glad Rags - One's best clothes
- Graybacks - Lice
- Grease the Track - to be run over by a train
- Gump - a scrap of meat
- Honey dipping - Working with a shovel in the sewer
- Hot - (1) A fugitive hobo. (2) A decent meal:
  "I could use three hots and a flop."
- Hot Shot - train with priority freight, stops rarely,
  goes faster. synonym for "Cannonball"
- Jungle - An area off a railroad where hobos camp and congregate
- Jungle Buzzard - a hobo or tramp who preys on their own
- Knowledge bus - A school bus used for shelter
- Main Drag - the busiest road in a town
- Moniker / Monica - A nickname
- Mulligan - a type of community stew created by several hobos
  combining whatever food they have or can collect
- Nickel note - five-dollar bill
- On The Fly - jumping a moving train
- Padding the hoof - to travel by foot
- Possum Belly - to ride on the roof of a passenger car.
  ne must lie flat, on his/her stomach, to not be blown off
- Pullman - a rail car
- Punk - any young kid
- Reefer - A compression of "refrigerator car".
- Road kid - A young hobo who apprentices himself to an older hobo
  in order to learn the ways of the road
- Road stake - the small amount of money a hobo may
  have in case of an emergency
- Rum dum - A drunkard
- Sky pilot - a preacher or minister
- Soup bowl- A place to get soup, bread and drinks
- Snipes - Cigarette butts "sniped" (eg. in ashtrays)
- Spear biscuits - Looking for food in garbage cans
- Stemming - panhandling or mooching along the streets
- Tokay Blanket - drinking alcohol to stay warm
- Yegg - A traveling professional thief

St. Pat's Rectory

St. Pat's Church

155

Phitty, Dad, Mom, Rita, Hezzie, Jim, Butch, Dewey, Babe, 1958

Levittown, 1969

156

A rare photo of all twelve siblings together in 1975

My dear sisters, Phyllis, Audrey and Rita, 1983

Taken the day of my Dad's funeral in 1983

Thompson Family Reunion 1985

On the steps of St. Pat's Church, 1991

Late 1990's – A gathering at Babe's house

Lakemont Park, 1999

Levittown, 1999

160

2002 – the "boys" in front of Babe's motor home after a day of salmon fishing

The love of my life

Our daughters – Sharon, Maureen, and Becky

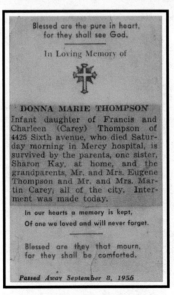

Blessed are the pure in heart,
for they shall see God.

In Loving Memory of

DONNA MARIE THOMPSON

Infant daughter of Francis and Charleen (Carey) Thompson of 4425 Sixth avenue, who died Saturday morning in Mercy hospital, is survived by the parents, one sister, Sharon Kay, at home, and the grandparents, Mr. and Mrs. Eugene Thompson and Mr. and Mrs. Martin Carey, all of the city. Interment was made today.

In our hearts a memory is kept,
Of one we loved and will never forget.

Blessed are they that mourn,
for they shall be comforted.

Passed Away September 8, 1956

Our Little Angel, Donna Marie
September 8, 1956

162

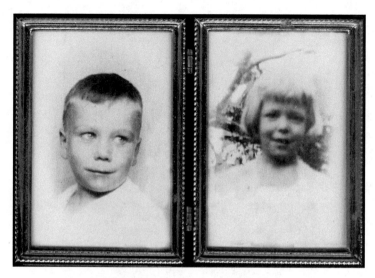

Hezzie & Charleen at 5 years old

Hezzie & Charleen

This journal has been completed with the assistance of many friends from my hometown who have supplied me not only with photos and historical background, but their own tales from the past; some I dare say even tainted with the truth!

Thanks also to my daughter Maureen and granddaughter Molly for the editing, research and compiling of facts and photos, in addition to the ongoing support from daughters Sharon and Becky.

A special thanks to my friend Angela Lynch, for all of her expert assistance.

To my granddaughter Allie, thanks again for suggesting, "Pap, let's write a story!" ...